The Ten Minute Activist

The Ten Minute Activist

Easy Ways to Take Back the Planet

The Mission Collective

Illustrated by Lloyd Dangle

Edited by
M Ryan Hess

NATION BOOKS
NEW YORK

THE TEN MINUTE ACTIVIST:
Easy Ways to Take Back the Planet

Published by
Nation Books
An Imprint of Avalon Publishing Group, Inc.
245 West 17th Street, 11th Floor
New York, NY 10011

AVALON
publishing group incorporated

Copyright © 2007 The Mission Collective
Illustrations copyright © 2007 Lloyd Dangle

Nation Books is a copublishing venture of the Nation Institute and Avalon Publishing
Group, Incorporated.

Library of Congress Cataloging-in-Publication Data is available.

ISBN-10: 1-56025-970-1
ISBN-13: 978-1-56025-970-1

9 8 7 6 5 4 3 2 1

Interior design by Maria E. Torres

Printed in Canada
Distributed by Publishers Group West

ENVIRONMENTAL BENEFITS STATEMENT

NEW LEAF
PAPER™

Avalon Publishing Group saved the following resources by using
New Leaf Paper, made with 100% recycled fiber and 40% post-
consumer waste, processed chlorine free.

trees	water	energy	solid waste	greenhouse gases
16 fully grown	6,850 gallons	17 million Btu	1,467 pounds	4,413 pounds

Calculations based on research by Environmental Defense and other members of the Paper Task Force.

 ©2006 New Leaf Paper   www.newleafpaper.com

Contents

Acknowledgments

THE MISSION COLLECTIVE thanks the good folks at Nation Books, Carl Bromley and Ruth Baldwin. We also thank Megan O'Patry, our star researcher and intern, for all her efforts. We want to thank Joshua Muscat and Bailey Salisbury for their contributions. Lastly, though it scarcely needs mentioning, we thank Elvis (the King).

Introduction

IT'S OFFICIAL. SIZE does matter.

Whether it's the size of the human population, the scale of our pollution, the extinction rate, or the distance between the haves and have-nots, humanity is screwing up, big time. All of this adds up to *big* trouble for planet Earth and its upstart species, *Homo sapiens*.

Are we too smart for our own good or not smart enough? Getting the answer wrong (or totally ignoring it) won't just destroy a city or a nation. The scope and breadth of our pressure on the planet is now big enough to put our very survival into question.

It turns out that a good way to address these big problems is by thinking small. We can no longer wait for governments or leaders to lead the way. It's up to individuals now.

This book is filled with small ideas that can be applied to your life and, collectively, result in big changes. Some of them will be familiar, others weird, some inspirational, and some perfect additions to your lifestyle. More than just facts, these are actions that will make a real difference.

Not everyone can do every action. But doing even one will make a noticeable improvement in your life. Moreover, others will notice your small acts, the fun you're having, and even the money you're saving: all of which is great PR for the cause.

That said, take your life down a notch today and take ten for the future.

Coal-Free Reading

CONSIDER THE LIGHTBULB shining over this book as you read. A mixture of energy sources generated that light. Most are polluting, and many add to global warming. If the by-products of producing that electricity accompanied the light into your home, your room would be filled with quite a toxic cocktail. Over half of the room would be polluted by coal by-products: sulfur dioxide, ozone, mercury, lead, cadmium, and chromium. Of that, 20 percent would be glowing with radioactivity from the nuke plants involved in generating the electricity. Another 20 percent would be filled with greenhouse gases from burning oil and natural gas. That leaves only 7 percent from hydroelectric power and a measly 2 percent of clean, pure air from renewables like solar and wind power.

Before you turn off the light and stop reading, there's something you can do. The U.S. Environmental Protection Agency (EPA) has two online tools that can help you see where your local energy comes from and how it compares to the rest of the United States. After you've used the first tool, the the Power Profiler, and decided you don't like your reading light raising sea levels for three-eyed fish, you can check out their second tool, the Green Power Locator. This shows you what green energy programs you can join in your area, to make your reading a little less polluting.

The Power Profiler can be found at www.epa.gov/powerprofiler/powerprofiler.htm; the Green Power Locator is at ww.epa.gov/green power/locator/index.htm.

Your Own Private Gaia

It creeps and crawls, slithers around in and out of the dirt, has feathers, fur, and cilia, and sometimes rows and rows of ears. It's that little plot of ecosystem out back: your garden.

A garden is a living entity, an association of living organisms distinct from one another yet dependent on each other for survival. Plants, birds, insects, bacteria, fungi, and mammals all play a role in creating the larger entity known as the garden.

Like any living organism, gardens need clean, toxin-free food and water in order to thrive. People have been farming organically for the past ten thousand years, but the modern emphasis on synthetic chemicals in farming only took off in 1939. In other words, energy-intensive products like chemical fertilizers and pesticides are very seldom needed if the soil is well tended. Composting organic waste from the kitchen is the best way to do this (see Compost Happens, p. 183). But composting from within the garden is also a good idea. In fact, throwing away weeds is probably the most common mistake people make. When weeds are removed, the overall nutrient level of the soil declines, thus reducing the nutritive value of the garden's food. But be careful, your compost heap must generate sufficient heat from the breaking down of organic matter in order to kill the weed seeds before you use weed compost.

So do like your great-great-great (to the 150th power) grandparents did, and go organic in the garden.

Clean Dry Cleaning

There are some things you just can't clean yourself, but did you know how horribly toxic traditional dry cleaning is? The Federal Clean Air Act says that perchloroethylene, the main dry cleaning chemical, is an environmentally hazardous air pollutant. When released into the environment through spills or sewage leaks, it ruins soil and groundwater, and poisons people, animals, and plants. It's hazardous to workers and neighbors, and is firmly linked to kidney damage, liver damage, and cancer. In fact, dry cleaning shops are declared toxic cleanup sites all the time. Now consider how many there are in your neighborhood.

In the past few years, though, there have been some real breakthroughs. Foremost among them is earth-friendly "wet cleaning" that uses computer-operated washing machines with special biodegradable soaps, conditioners, and finishers.

According to the EPA, wet cleaning works at least as well as dry cleaning. And it costs about the same to start and run a wet cleaner, so it shouldn't cost you extra. A bonus is that wet cleaning creates skilled jobs. Plus, it's more kind to your clothes, which saves you bucks in the long run.

Another alternative to dry cleaning uses carbon dioxide as a solvent. CO_2 is cheap, energy-efficient, reusable, abundant (it's an industrial by-product), and is much less toxic than perchloroethylene. Again, it should cost about the same as traditional dry cleaning.

So the next time you need a professional cleaner, scout around for one who doesn't use perchloroethylene. And take the time to let your current cleaner know that you'll be back as a customer when they go wet.

The Ocean on the Ropes

It's the match of the century! In the left corner, weighing in at a colossal gazillion tons, the wet-nurse of the world: the ocean! And in the right corner, standing billions strong, the dragon of drift nets: human industry!

Who will win? Nobody can tell. But it's the twelfth round and the ocean is looking pretty frazzled. Human industry has pummeled the life out of the ocean with 150-mile-long low-blow drift nets. We've raked her body with longlines, each with ten thousand left hooks apiece. And as if that weren't enough, toxic runoff from our communities has contaminated the whole ring, ending up in the ocean's fish and ultimately in our own bodies.

But as Rocky Balboa or Muhammad Ali could tell you, the underdog in the ring always has a twelfth-round comeback. In the ocean's case, that last-minute defense might lead to a total knockout of human civilization. The collapse of the ocean ecosystem has been measurable since 2000 and continues at 3 percent a year. At the same time, heavy metals have made some species dangerous to eat. Considering that one out of six people on Earth get their protein from fish, that could be one big thud against the mat, very soon.

We must learn to fish and consume responsibly, cutting out endangered and poisoned species. Check out the Monterey Bay Aquarium's Seafood Watch Web site to get updated info on what is and *is not* okay to eat in your area at www.mbayaq.org/cr/ seafoodwatch.asp. If you fish, check out the FDA's local fish advisories at www.epa.gov/waterscience/ fish/states.htm.

High-Cost Free Checking

There are two surprises waiting for you in your bank statement. The first is that your savings account broke the five-dollar mark! But before you crack open a celebratory beer, you better check out the second surprise: The bank has charged you $2.50 for that cash advance in Canada, $4 for ATM withdrawals at unaffiliated ATMs, and $10 for that cashier's check. Ever feel like the people hiding behind the bulletproof glass are laughing all the way to the . . . well, you know.

Hidden fees can add up quickly, earning banks $55 billion in 2006. But did you know that banks also make money by reinvesting your money in schemes that might turn your stomach more than even the surcharges? Some international banking firms are direct investors in defense and weapons systems and have their greedy little fingers in all sorts of unsavory multinational pots.

Instead of underwriting the fat cats, try searching out a credit union instead. Credit unions are essentially co-ops, owned by the folks who bank there and offering similar services as banks. You can get a credit card, open a checking account, or take out loans, but often at fairer rates and with lower fees. And unlike banks, credit unions do not operate for profit. They are a convenience offered to anyone who qualifies. Who qualifies? Usually employees of certain companies or organizations, but sometimes residents of a region. You can call the Credit Union National Association to find a potential credit union to match your profile at (800) 358-5710.

The Plastic Jesus Revolution

Here's a bumper sticker for you: *How would Jesus manage?* Ernest Bader, a British plastics company owner, asked himself that very question in 1951. Americans, accustomed to the rugged individualism espoused for nearly a century by the Christian Right, might be surprised by Bader's answer.

Bader envisioned applying Christian principles of fellowship, social responsibility, and charity to his firm, while remaining profitable and serving as an acceptable model to other companies. The result was the Scott Bader Commonwealth, an employee-owned entity, forced to live within certain limits, to reroute 5 percent of its profits to charities, and to never sell to customers involved in war-related industries.

Today, Bader's Commonwealth is called the Scott Bader Company. Even in this age of corporate scandals and Chapter 11 pension dismemberment, Ernest Bader's company, and its ethical business model, has spread across Europe, to the Middle East, and to the United States. Each of its units remains limited in size, fully employee owned, and continues to follow the sense of social responsibility outlined by Ernest Bader . . . while making a buck (or a quid).

Take a few minutes today to visit the Scott Bader Web site at www.scottbader.com to learn more about their history, principles, and successes. Then take a look at your own company or workplace and ask yourself, how would Jesus restructure?

Eating on Time

A GROUP OF inner-city schoolchildren once went to the forests of Point Reyes National Seashore in California and were perplexed. Many had never been outside their impoverished neighborhood, let alone entered a forest. One asked the park ranger: "How far down do you have to dig before you get to the concrete?"

Before we laugh (or cry), we might consider our own alienation from the natural order of things. Take the electric lights that allow night to become day and air-conditioning that can transform summer into spring. Our food habits are also out of sync with nature. Do you know when to plant corn seeds? Or when to harvest garlic? Few of us do.

Our modern life, unlike most of the world, is now almost entirely independent from the seasons. But eating this way comes at a cost. A ripe tomato in January has to be grown far from your winter home, or in an energy-intensive greenhouse. That requires burning fossil fuels to grow and ship the tomato to your market. That same tomato could be produced locally and efficiently if it were grown in season.

Eating with the seasons (even just a little) can

benefit you, your community, and the environment. It reduces CO_2 emissions needed to grow and transport food. It benefits your local farmers, who have fresh, in-season crops to offer you. And it also saves money, since out-of-season food costs more. But most importantly, in-season food is more nutritious because it's fresher.

To learn about what foods are in season, check out the British Web site www.eattheseasons.co.uk. A North American version is due to launch by 2007.

Good to the Last Drop of Blood

"America is addicted to oil." President Bush finally owned up to that one in his 2006 State of the Union speech. But there's another "black gold" Americans are addicted to and, like oil, it costs lives.

The United States consumes more coffee than any other nation on the planet. It's our second-largest import in fact, second only to, you guessed it, oil. But how and why does coffee cost lives? To start, in 1989 the United States succeeded in abolishing the International Coffee Agreement, which stabilized prices, in favor of free trade policies. Prices quickly plummeted from $1.20 per pound in the 1980s to 41 cents per pound today. This was a boon for the giant coffee corporations, who used their control of the market to force farmers to accept the lower prices while not passing on the savings to consumers. In countries like Mexico and El Salvador, tens of thousands of coffee farmers have lost their livelihoods and even face starvation because of the deregulated coffee market. In West Africa, farmers must use slave labor in order to function. Meanwhile, the coffee giants have soaked up huge profits.

You can opt out of this dirty business by searching for cafes and grocery stores that carry coffee produced under fair and legal labor conditions. Look for the Free Trade Certified label to ensure your caffeine comes without strings attached. Plus, more of your coffee money will go to the growers and laborers as opposed to the corporate middlemen.

If your local area hasn't caught on yet, fair trade coffee is available online at www.globalexchange.org.

Manufacturing Peace

Know how to meditate? For ten minutes, sit still, close your eyes, and concentrate on your breathing while allowing intrusive thoughts to float by like fluffy little clouds. The first few times may not be completely effortless, but it pays to persevere, since the health benefits are incredible. People who meditate regularly experience lowered heart rate, blood pressure, and cholesterol; a reduction in stress, anxiety and depression; fewer headaches; better sleep; and a nice, peaceful feeling that David Lynch likes to call "bliss."

And he should know. Our favorite surreal director has been meditating daily for thirty-two years and has big plans to establish seven peace factories where fifty thousand advanced meditators can promote peace in the world by producing a state totally lacking in negativity, affecting the environment around them. The transcendental meditation movement has documented a reduced crime rate in areas where groups of meditators are concentrated—including Washington, D.C., in the early 1990s, so it looks very possible that doing nothing at all may well be the best road to global harmony. At the very least, your own little dominion will flourish as your serenity spreads outward to those you love.

Yes Means No

Is playing dress-up enough to get you noticed? It is if you accessorize with fake IDs and thrift-store business suits and have the *cajones* to take the media and global business by the horns and ride them silly. Such is the story of the Yes Men—Andy Bichlbaum and Mike Bonanno.

The Yes Men became famous pranksters in 1999, when they helped put www.gwbush.com, a parody Web site of the real Bush election site, online. Encouraged by a public rebuke from Bush himself, the Yes Men aimed their satirical eyes on the WTO through a new Web site, www.gatt.org. Many people mistook www.gatt.org for the real McCoy and invited the Yes Men to deliver speeches. They gladly accepted, mercilessly implicating the WTO in outrageous statements in the process.

Their career highlights include: announcing a WTO scheme to take human waste from the first world and turn it into third world fast food; declaring the U.S. Civil War a waste of time, since globalization has brought slavery back anyway; being interviewed on TV by CNBC and the BBC (as WTO spokesmen); and even declaring a mea culpa to a business audience for all the wrong the WTO has done, and then announcing the WTO would be closing up shop in disgrace.

It's been a wild party. And you're invited to join. For a free lesson on how to be a Yes Man or Woman, visit www.theyesmen.org.

Reading between the Headlines

Every morning, former President John F. Kennedy insisted on reading six different newspapers with breakfast. Obviously, with his daily intelligence briefing, Kennedy was not short on news stories. But he read the papers anyway to get a sense of what Americans were being told as compared with what he was being told.

We don't all have the time or inclination to digest several news sources with our coffee every day. But if we value being well informed, it's important to learn what every journalist is taught in school: all news has a bias and can be told in many different ways.

So how does one become a savvy news consumer?

Our recipe goes like this. Relying on one source is bland, especially if that source always presents the arguments you want to hear. Put your *Nation* magazine chocolate in your McLaughlin Group peanut butter. And add a little foreign newspaper zest, since there can be glaring differences between the domestic and foreign press. And don't forget to sprinkle online chat rooms and blogs into the mix. Bloggers sometimes expose stories the big media groups won't touch; just ask ousted Republican Majority Leader Trent Lott of Mississippi, whose racist remarks were picked up by bloggers.

For a little variety, we offer these six delicious news sources.

- Alternet: www.alternet.org
- Congressional Quarterly: www.cq.com (what the fat cats read)
- GNN (Guerrilla News Network): www. guerrillanews.com

- Google News: www.news.google.com
  (news supplied by 4,500 news sources)
- Independent Media Center: www.indymedia.org
- Tom Dispatch: www.tomdispatch.com

Tofu or Not Tofu? That Is the Question

As one of India's holiest cities, Varanasi is not only a great place to die, it's also a great place to be a cow. The benevolent bovine is considered holy in India, and in Varanasi, cows (literally) have the run of the city's narrow streets. And because they're holy, they don't have to worry about being served up as beef curry.

Vegetarianism dates back millennia in India and was even popularized in the West for its spiritual qualities by India's Mahatma Gandhi. Today, there are at least two more reasons to go vegetarian, or at least become more vegetarian: the selfish argument and the big picture argument.

We'll start with the big picture. Producing meat for the world's growing billions of mouths is taking a big toll on the Earth. A Cornell study showed that producing meat protein is eight times more energy intensive than producing vegetable protein. And a University of Chicago study showed that 6 percent of U.S. greenhouse emissions come from the extra energy used to produce meat.

Now, the selfish argument: your health can be improved by eating a more vegetarian diet. There's one caveat, though. A strict vegetarian diet requires careful planning in order to get all the iron, B-12, and other nutrients your body needs. Still, even part-time vegetarianism pays off for the environment, your body, and the cows. So, take a little time today to come up with a one-day vegetarian menu. Bon appétit!

Just Ride,
She Said

On June 27, 1997, the summer fog chilled San Francisco to the bone, its mayor, Willie Brown, was hot under the collar. Why? The mayor's car was stuck in a little more traffic than usual, on account of 3,500 bicyclists also sharing the road. Stating that "Enough is enough," Mayor Brown vowed to crush the city's monthly bicycle ride, known as Critical Mass, which had interrupted his car trip. In response to such rhetoric, bicyclists from across the region converged on the city for the following month's Critical Mass, shutting down the city's streets in a popular two-wheeled uprising.

As one of the myriad, unofficial Web sites of Critical Mass attests, there is no organization called Critical Mass. Rather, it is a spontaneous monthly ride in which groups of bicyclists take to the streets en masse to promote bicycling, get some exercise, and, more than anything else, have a good time. Critical Mass rides have sprung up across the planet in hundreds of cities, from Tokyo to Johannesburg and from London to Rio de Janeiro.

You can see if there is already a ride in your town by doing a search online. One resource is www.critical-mass.org, but it's hardly the only list. If you don't find one, you can start one yourself. Just do what the people in San Francisco did in 1992: call up a group of friends and start riding.

Seeing the Light

This book is all about little lightbulbs going off in your head. But while you're at it, how about making your bright ideas fluorescent? Regular lightbulbs are just bad news, wasting costly electricity on heat rather than light. Compact fluorescent bulbs, however, produce the same light for less than 25 percent of the energy. So while you ease up on the juice, you can ease up on global warming and energy pollution at the same time. Plus, you can save dough.

Compact fluorescent bulbs are small and screw into a regular socket. And they're not necessarily going to turn your living room into a blue-lit office-from-hell. Today, you can buy fluorescent lights that cast a pleasing, warm white light that looks the same as regular bulbs.

Before you race out to fill up on fluorescents, here are some facts to keep in mind. Lumens measure light. Watts measure energy. When shopping, find the most lumens for the least watts. Also, while some compact fluorescents contain a tiny trace of mercury, it's less than the mercury released by burning the amount of fossil fuel they'll save. So, they're still a much better deal. But that means you must dispose of them properly. Check with your local recycling center.

The days of long, buzzing, headache-causing tubes are over. Rejoice with a curly, quiet coil of light!

Repent, O Shopper!

The devil's loose in America! He sits on a big box with a royal carpet of blacktop smothering our towns. He's got a red, white, and blue twinkle in his dark eyes and the seeds of economic ruin in his pocket.

But in the devil's hour of triumph, a light has come to vanquish the great deceiver. With a lot of blond hair and a white suit, he's gonna give that devil a good preachin'-to.

Ever since his itinerant days on Times Square, Reverend Billy and his Church of Stop Shopping have been making pilgrimages to Wal-Marts, shopping malls, shareholder meetings, Starbucks, and every other playground of the evil one. Coming along on this joyride of consumer salvation is his Stop Shopping Gospel Choir, composed of credit card debtors, bicycle criminals, and former Solid Gold dancers—all raising their voices to put the "odd back in God."

The reverend is an honest-to-god gospel preacher (with a little Jerry Lee Lewis thrown in), preaching to corporate America to change its ways. He's also got his wild eyes on all us sinners. In December

2005 he traveled to malls across the country to save Christmas from the "shopocalypse"! And last year he "confronted" the Victoria's Secret shareholders annual meeting. Their catalogs come from virgin boreal forests.

You can learn more about the Church, watch their videos, and find out when they will be in your community next at www.revbilly.com. Join now or burn in shopper's hell.

Hand Tool Wisdom

Attention, all you green thumbs out there! It's time to get even greener.

Gardening might be calming, rewarding, and even fun, but cut out the gas-guzzling power tools, and your garden hobby just became actual work. And as a famous frog once sang: "It ain't easy being . . ." well, you know.

If you're already enthusiastic about better lawns

and gardens, you may not mind burning calories and building up muscles in an effort to spare the air. But if machine-free gardening still sounds like onerous toiling in the fields, check out these factoids. Most gasoline-powered lawn and garden tools, such as lawn mowers, weed whackers, and leaf blowers, are extremely eco-unfriendly, spewing an incredible amount of CO_2 into the air, even considering their small stature. In fact, a single lawn mower can put out more pollution than seventy-three new cars. That adds up to as much as 5 percent of urban air pollution. In a single day, Southern California's lawn tools do more to pollute the air than every airplane in Los Angeles.

Fortunately, there are tools available that are more environmentally friendly, more ergonomic, and even more efficient. Push mowers aren't nearly as unruly and cumbersome as the one that earned you your childhood allowance. This goes for pretty much all necessary lawn and garden tools. You can dispense with the leaf blower by using a simple broom and rake. Or, you can ditch the power hedger and get intimate with your plants by using a pair of pruning scissors. One final bonus is that it's easier on the ears for you and your neighbors.

And remember, ye shall reap what ye shall sow. So sow some peace and quiet, and a little fresh air this weekend.

Sharing the Load

San Francisco Bay Area suburbanites have many ways to get to work using public transportation. There are public trains, buses, and taxis. And then there's going in style. Some will get picked up by a Lexus and some by a Ferrari, and some will be transported within the comfort and roominess of a leather-seated Caddie. What kind of public transit system is this, you ask? Why, it's none other than the Bay Area's Casual Carpool system. Getting a ride is as easy as standing at designated street corners where commuters wait for drivers going their way.

Carpooling just makes sense, even if it's only part-time. When we share rides, we save gas and highway and bridge tolls, and in some areas we get to use carpool lanes. We also cut down on wear and tear on our own cars. Plus, we reduce pollution and dependence on foreign oil.

Even if your area doesn't sponsor official carpool stops, you can still share the load, and maybe even make some friends. Whether you do it through work or through the Internet, car pools are readily available to most commuters.

Two online ways to find your new carpool buddies are www.erideshare.com and www.carpool connect. com.

TV Shutdown Week

In 1973, the first one-eyed monsters arrived in a
sleepy Canadian town. Right behind them was Tannis
Williams, a University of British Columbia researcher.
Williams's goal: to study the effects of TV on the

community. His findings: violence among the town's children increased 160 percent.

Thirty years on, a slew of studies draw the same conclusion: television breeds trouble, especially for children who witness almost eight violent acts an hour, twice the adult rate if you include the cartoons they watch. Now consider that American boob tubes stay on seven hours a day. Not surprisingly, there's also an epidemic of obesity.

It may be impossible to totally kill your TV, but you can certainly experiment. Try joining the twenty-four million folks who participate in TV-Turnoff Week by unplugging your TV for one week. If it's on right now, get up and unplug it. And don't fret; you only have seven days to go. If you only watch the news and a rerun of *Seinfeld* or *The Simpsons* every day, you just earned yourself several hours of free time. That's more time for reading, exercise, "slow meals," hobbies, friends and family, and especially more time for sex with your partner!

Oh, and even though you'll certainly face a two-foot-tall revolt, remember to include your children in the TV turnoff. They'll get more exercise and homework done. And if you work in a day care center, unplug the TV there, too, since 70 percent of them use TVs daily.

To learn more about TV-Turnoff Week, visit www.tvturnoff.org.

The Other Red Meat

For many Americans, red meat is a kind of soul food. Even declared vegetarians will break down and have a burger now and then. Yet the production of beef is one of the most destructive activities for our environment. The total world cattle population is now approximately 1.3 billion, occupying some 24 percent of the land of the planet and causing devastating destruction to tropical rain forests in South America. Currently half the water consumed in the United States is used to grow grain for cattle feed. On top of this, cattle are almost universally pumped full of growth stimulants, hormones, and antibiotic-laced feed, all of which end up in our own systems.

So what's a red meat lover to do? Take a tip from cowboy mogul Ted Turner, who owns the largest buffalo ranch in the United States, and switch to America's *original* red meat.

Meat from bison is highly nutrient dense, due to the per-calorie proportion of protein, fat, minerals, and essential fatty acids. *Reader's Digest* has even listed bison as one of the five foods women should eat regularly for its high iron content. And look, Mom, no antibiotics or hormones!

Bison don't require deforestation. The Great Plains were originally filled with the hearty, low-maintenance creatures, who don't eat as much as cattle. And the taste is pretty similar to beef. Bison is already popular in cities like Denver, Chicago, and

San Francisco, so if your city doesn't stock it, stampede up to your butcher's counter and demand some.

Choosing Sides

Greens are at war with one another . . . and sometimes with themselves. The heart of the controversy is so fundamental to energy, the environment, and natural resource conservation, that few thoughtful people escape entrapment in its sticky nuances. What could possibly trip so many up? Why, none other than the mother of all decisions: which packaging is best—glass or plastic?

Many choose glass for its "natural" qualities. But plastic proponents will point out, truthfully, that it takes more energy to make virgin glass than plastic. Yet, all plastic is made of petroleum—bane of the green movement. And when you consider that Americans use 2.5 million plastic bottles each and every hour, you can imagine how much oil is wasted.

Glass advocates should remember, however, that their preference is made of limited resources, too: silica, potash, and lime. And, like plastic, Americans throw away a lot of glass: about thirteen million tons each year. And for each ton of glass made, nearly four hundred pounds of mining waste is generated.

The only clear answer, then, is that no matter which we use, glass or plastic, recycling is crucial. Plastic is easily recycled into more plastic, saving 80 percent of the energy needed for new plastic. And plastics can be recycled repeatedly. Recycling glass saves 50 percent of the energy used for producing new glass, and most kinds of glass can be recycled endlessly. So, take sides if you will, but be sure to agree that recycling is the common answer.

Slow the Flow

As we note later in Give Me Shower or Give Me Death (p. 61), a good, hot, blasting shower can make your whole day. But it can also use double the amount of water that you actually need. In fact, showers and sinks are the biggest water wasters in most homes.

Low-flow showerheads and faucet aerators (the doohickeys that screw onto the end of your faucet) are the first and best way to save water in your home. It's a snap to save up to 60 percent on your water—and for shower-time opera singers, that can be a tremendous amount. With a low-flow showerhead, a five-minute shower will use less than 12.5 gallons. With an old-school showerhead you'd use up to 50 gallons! Aerators work comparable magic.

Aerators and low-flow showerheads are imprinted with their rates. If your showerhead is more than 2.5 gallons per minute (GPM), or if your aerators are old and plugged up with grit, get new ones. Current aerators offer as low as a 0.5 GPM.

For those traumatized by a bad experience with a low-flow showerhead: it's true that a lot of them used to be lame, but today's models now have excellent pressure. Best of all, it's a quick fix, and you don't need to sweat over the cost. You'll save gallons of liquidity on water and water heating in no time.

Interest Payments in Your Own Interest

Here's how the system works. You go to the local hardware store, stock up on energy-saving lightbulbs, a composting system, and a bicycle pump using your bank card. A month later, you make your monthly payment, which winds its way from your bank account to your creditor, who donates the money to the political action committee of a rapacious, antienvironmental politician. Sound counterproductive? It doesn't have to be, if you choose your creditor wisely.

Whether its financing illegal logging, charging minorities higher interest rates, practicing predatory banking, or funding opponents to green candidates, the banking, and credit industry have a lot of explaining to do these days. Several consumer and environmental groups have filed lawsuits and published studies on the exploits of some of the United States' biggest banks. For up-to-date information, the Rain Forest Action Network and the Center for Responsible Lending are great sources.

Luckily, your money talks. If you don't like how your creditor is investing, you can take your business to a green merchant. There are plenty of them out there. Credit unions are your best bet (see High-Cost Free Checking, p. 10). They often market themselves for their community reinvestment and proactive investing policies. You can also try the highly successful Working Assets Visa card, which has generated $6 million in donations to worthy causes. There are as many choices as there are points of view. Take a few minutes today to make your money work *for* you instead of against you.

Waste Not, Want Not

IT'S NEVER BEEN easier to be the ultimate wasteoid. Our stores offer ample opportunity to buy single-use, throwaway items like paper napkins, plastic food wrap, disposable diapers, throwaway cameras, plastic pens, disposable razors, etc. And more and more of our consumer products are designed with an intentionally short life span, such as tea kettles with heat-intolerant plastic handles and soft-soled shoes.

Luckily, we have the choice of opting out of the throwaway culture. Each of the items above has a perfectly reusable alternative. And when we add durability to the mix, we are buying one item for life, saving energy, money, and landfill space in the process.

Still, even the most throwaway-intolerant among us has a few throwaway items in their home. But by thinking creatively, we can find new uses for throwaway items before they depart for the landfill. The incredible, evolving sponge is one example.

It begins in the kitchen, cleaning our plates. Later, as the sponge starts to wear, it is promoted to kitchen counter detail. Eventually, our old sponge gets stinky and is placed in charge of our floor. Finally, the sponge is given a humble retirement in the bathroom, cleaning the toilet until that solemn day comes when the venerable house cleaner's life sees one stain too many. Be sure to mark the sponge every time it moves to a new stage to avoid unsavory mix-ups.

You can also save a lot of energy and material by reusing the jars and bottles your food comes in. Use an old liquor bottle for sauces and dressings. Or transform a plastic peanut butter jar into a home for leftovers.

However you do it, there's lots of opportunity to reduce your impact by buying reusables for durability and using throwaway items smartly.

Down with Free Trade Bullies

These days, you can't throw a brick without hitting some globalization guru or political patsy jaw-jacking at full volume about "free trade." That's greed-speak for a host of horrors like third-world sweatshops, wholesale ecocide, puppet regimes, wars on indigenous peoples, forced prison labor, and child slavery.

Think back to when you were a kid. Even as a squirt, you knew that there was no life form worse than someone who tried to force an unfair trade. You learned that the first time someone bigger, stronger, and meaner swiped your chocolate pudding for his carrot sticks.

Nowadays, the unfair trade bullies run around in boardrooms and legislatures. They wave the flag with one hand while signing unfair trade treaties like GATT, NAFTA, and FTAA with the other. Meanwhile, these agreements largely overlook labor abuses so Western shopping malls can sell bargain-priced widgets.

In reality, free trade is not free, but fair trade is always fair. When you buy fair trade products, you're assured the workers were paid well and treated decently. You can help support fair trade by going out to the store of your choice and asking what fair trade–certified items they have. If they don't have any, tell them why you want some. If they have some, buy them. But remember, fair trade costs more. You wouldn't have traded pudding for carrots, so why should you trade widgets for freedom? Talk truth to marketplace bullies; buy a fair trade product today.

The Less Gassy Driver

Sammy Hagar may not be able to drive fifty-five, but he's burning a lot of unnecessary gas. According to recent car tests, driving fifty-five mph is still the most efficient highway speed, reducing gasoline usage by as much as 14 percent. If you drive sixty-five mph, it will cost you only ten minutes of your time, and you might actually get there!

Speed, however, is not the best gas-saving trick. Driving more calmly by breaking easier and accelerating more slowly makes the biggest difference: more than 30 percent. So, when you have to drive, keep your attention on the road, far ahead, giving yourself more time to brake. Similarly, when you accelerate, use a light foot, taking your time to get up to speed.

Two other ways include using cruise control (saving up to 14 percent gas) and turning your car off when you expect to idle longer than one minute (saving as much as another 19 percent). If you follow all these tips, you could save roughly a third of the gasoline that the maniac swerving in and out of traffic is using. All that savings translates not just into money, but also into CO_2 you're not adding to the atmosphere.

So if you don't have a rock star's budget, or his need for speed, test-drive these recommendations today. There's even a special lane for you—the one on the far right.

Home of the Brave

We'll call him Bruce. On a bad day, he has to brave the sadistic taunts of the devils behind the Dumpster.

On a good day, he has the wherewithal to seek shelter and food. Bruce, like a quarter of the homeless in the United States, is part of the group that is hardest to help, suffering from a mental disability and unable to maintain stable housing. But there are many faces to homelessness. Not all have mental disabilities. Many are employed, a quarter are women, and 42 percent—the fastest growing segment—are families with children.

The U.S. Census Bureau doesn't even try to count the homeless, but estimates put the number at around three quarters of a million people. Communities have responded in different ways. Thirty percent of cities, including Atlanta and Dallas, have simply pushed the problem onto others, by banning panhandling. Others, like San Francisco and New York, have more proactive policies that have made significant dents in the problem. But in the richest country in the world, the homeless population remains.

On an individual basis, there are many ways to

respond. Treating the homeless as human beings is a start. Small acts of kindness, like smiling or even shaking hands, can do a great deal of good. Setting aside portions of your oversized restaurant dish is often well received by the folks outside. And, if your town has a homeless newspaper program, buy a copy from a homeless person and check it out.

Old McDonald Had a House of Horrors

Right or wrong, healthy or not, most of us eat meat— and some of us eat a lot of meat. But with mad cow disease, injectable growth goop, and other issues, it's extra smart to know where your meat is coming from.

Most of us, if we had the choice, wouldn't eat meat if it came from an abused animal. While it's nice to think that our chicken or lamb lived a happy life on a cute farm, it probably didn't, even if the package says "free-range."

Free-range rules are more like guidelines. Take free-range chicken. While you're insisting on free-range chicken, lots of huge "free-range" farms are insisting on cramming a zillion chickens into one room with a tiny opening that lets just few outside. The birds are still standing in their mess and trying to kill each other with cruelly amputated beaks. Cows, pigs, turkeys, and lambs don't have it any better.

But wait, it gets worse. "Certified organic," "cage-free," "free-roaming," and "vegetarian-fed" labels don't mean the animal wasn't mutilated, starved, or otherwise abused. However, guilty meat lovers don't have to go cold turkey. An up-and-coming standard called "Certified Humane Raised and Handled" is being developed. Talk to the store or meat department boss about this label and why it means so much. You can also contact Humane Farm Animal Care at (703) 435-3883 or go to www.certified humane.org tp find a shop in your town that sells certified humane products.

Please Don't Feed
the Animals

EVER WONDER WHY your trash has been singled out by raccoons, rodents, or bears? It's not that these animals necessarily prefer eating trash to their regular diets. It's just that sloppy and insufficient garbage disposal and/or human encroachment into the animals' natural habitat makes it so damn easy. But the damage extends far beyond an unwelcome guest in the middle of the night or a garbage-strewn lawn. To protect people from garbage-hunting bears, local authorities often destroy the animal rather than risk a future human casualty. Human garbage only encourages them to view your residence as a reliable food source.

At home, always seal garbage cans tight so they cannot easily be pried open. Most animals will be attracted by the smell of food, whether there is any left or not. Keeping them from investigating the inside of your trash containers will keep them from returning. Same goes for camping. *Nothing* (including toothpaste or lotions) should be left out to attract wild animals.

Food packaging is also a concern. That Coors Lite six-pack ring casually thrown into the sea or onto the beach will last 450 *years* in seawater. That's plenty of time for a bird or sea creature to find it and either try to eat it or get entangled in it. Plastic bags are often mistaken for one of the favorite meals of sea turtles: jellyfish.

On your next camping or fishing trip, or your next visit to the garbage can, "lock and load" for your animal friends.

Going Native in the Garden

The Irish potato famine made monoculture famous. Monoculture is where farmers grow only one species of crop. In the case of nineteenth-century Ireland, growing one species of potato allowed a single strain of potato blight to destroy that nation's spud crop, leading to the starvation of a million Irish and the exodus of many more refugees.

And monoculture is alive and well today. In fact, thanks to the consolidation of global agribusiness firms, monoculture is booming. According to the Action Group on Erosion, Technology and Concentration, just ten companies control half of the world's seeds. These companies go to great lengths to expand their market share by pushing their seeds on more and more farmers. In the process, these companies are pushing out traditional varieties, leading to a dangerous lack of diversity in the world's food supply.

Many groups have sought to maintain traditional varieties of seeds. And the best way to save them is to plant them. Because many are native to your area, they can be perfectly suited to your local climate. They're also a great way to make your own garden into a biodiversity preserve.

The Native Seeds Search is one resource for traditional seeds. On their Web site, www.nativeseeds. org, you can buy folk seeds grown by Native American communities for centuries, such as the decorative devil's claw or the drought-tolerant blue speckled tepary bean. You can also find heirloom seed varieties at many independent nurseries and farmers' markets.

Give Me Shower or Give Me Death

If you're like most people, the shower is *the* single greatest indulgence you can't do without. It's not just about cleanliness. It's about having one moment a day when everything is guaranteed to be wonderful. You may tolerate shortfalls in other parts of life, but damn it, you'll never go without that shower!

Unfortunately, erasing all those worries relies on a lot of power from the local power plant, and that leads to something called global warming. If your household is like most, heating water accounts for 20 percent of your electric bill each month. But you don't have to ruin your life with shorter showers or cold plunges. Below are some baby steps to curb your water heater's appetite for electricity.

- Have a look to see if your water heater bears the "Energy Star" label. If not, it's probably time for a new one. Don't worry about cost—an energy-efficient water heater will pay for itself within two years.
- If your residence is equipped with an automatic electric dishwasher, set the temperature of your water heater to no higher than 140 degrees Fahrenheit. If you hand-wash your dishes, you can afford to turn it down to 120 degrees.
- If your water heater is located in an unheated area, insulate the heater and the surrounding pipes. Of course, consult your safety manual before doing this.
- You can set the water heater on a timer so that it operates only when you need it.

Calling All Lawbreakers

Is calling your lawmaker a *lawbreaker* a cheap shot? Well, it certainly doesn't cost a $1,000-a-plate dinner or a golfing trip to Scotland to do so. But with the epidemic of back-scratching in government today, it's hard to know the difference.

However you feel about politicians, there are times when we all must give them a piece of our minds. Two good ways to do so are phone calls and paper letters. E-mail is easiest, of course, but it's considered the least effective method.

To reach the offices of your congressman/woman, call the U.S. Capitol Switchboard at (202) 224-3121. In case you don't know your representative or senator's names, you can go to www.senate.gov or www.house.gov to find out.

If you do make a phone call, try these tips:

- Give your name and city, the issue in question, and ask to speak with the legislative assistant. Obviously Ted Kennedy and Bill Frist are, you know, too busy working for, um, the people to take the call personally.

- As sarcastic as that last statement was, always be extremely courteous and polite. Otherwise, you'll be labeled a crackpot and either ignored or put on some Travis Bickle watch list.

- Be prepared: have notes, including the bill number and where the politician stands.

- Finally, ask for a written response regarding your phone call that addresses how the congressman/woman is planning to act regarding this issue. Be sure to provide your full mailing address.

Old School

The next time you're in line at the store, look over the impulse-buy magazines and note the numerous ways in which they tell you to "feel younger!" or "lose 10 years in 10 minutes!" If you think about it, the only time anyone ever tries to look older is when they're too young to buy beer.

But hang on a sec. If we look at all the things we take for granted every day, most of them were built by older people. Your CD player? Never would have happened without pioneers who are now past retirement age. That cool old Mustang? Designed by someone on the job in 1965!

Fact is, older people are our data banks. They've actually taken the time to learn things that the rest of us haven't been able to figure out yet. They've tried more things, passed and failed more tests, and been through global wars and tribulations that would make short work of any contestant on *Survivor*.

What it comes down to is this: There's a cultural slant against older people in our country. We say they're cute, or annoying, or silly, or slow. But most of the time we don't say that they're seasoned, successful, smart, or sensitive. In short, we act as if they're not fully human.

But it's not hard to take another tack. All you have to do is ask. Take a moment today and chat up a senior in your life. They'd undoubtedly appreciate the rare spectacle of an interested young inquisitor.

Wonder Cures

They were the treasures buried with Neanderthals sixty thousand years ago. They're the bane of vampires. And one of the best solutions for the common cold. They're humanity's oldest cure-all: medicinal plants.

The majority of the world still relies on herbal medicine. But in the West, industrialized societies have largely turned away from plants in favor of synthetically made compounds controlled by doctors and Big Pharma companies.

At the same time, life is more hectic and more toxic than ever. The use of herbal medicine is one way you can help your body get back into a natural rhythm of health . . . and take back control of your health care.

Below are a few favorites of Western herbalist Joshua Muscat:

- Skullcap: great for relaxing the nervous system and muscle tension, without being sedating. Use two teaspoons of dry herbs in a cup of hot water, or take twenty to sixty drops of the tincture.
- Lomatium: useful for the cold or flu. It can be taken as a tincture (thirty drops every three hrs).
- Reishi mushroom: calms the mind and body, strengthens the immune system, regulates the circulatory system, and strengthens the lungs. It may be taken as a tea (ten slices simmered in one quart of water for forty-five minutes). Usually taken daily for two to six months.

- Vitex: regulates estrogen and progesterone in women. Eases menstrual cramps, menopausal hot flashes, and other hormonal imbalances. The tincture is taken as thirty to fifty drops three times per day.

The Answer Is Blowing in the Wind

Ah, Japan in springtime! Women shuffling between tea parties in kimonos, the sipping of sake under the cherry blossoms, the wind blowing through the laundry hung out to dry.

While it may have gone out of fashion in the United States, much of the world still hangs its laundry out to dry. Go anywhere in Japan and you can't help but notice the huge apartment buildings fluttering with drying clothes.

Clothes dryers are one of the biggest energy consumers in our homes, just after heaters, air conditioners, and clothes washers. Yet, during much of the year, most people could use alternative energy dryers—the sun and air. Both are delivered directly to your house daily for free. And, unlike machine dryers, air-drying doesn't rely on power stations emitting greenhouse gases.

Of course, many people like the sanitizing action of a machine dryer. But partially drying your clothes in the dryer before hanging them out has the same effect, at much less energy cost. You can also save energy by drying light items separately from jeans and heavy towels. For those without much extra space, like the Japanese, or if you consider hanging laundry an eyesore, buy a drying rack to put in a warm, out-of-the-way spot inside.

A word of warning, though. Many neighborhoods actually ban clotheslines. Check out the folks at www.laundrylist.org, who celebrate hanging clothes. They even have an online gallery of artwork based on the clothesline.

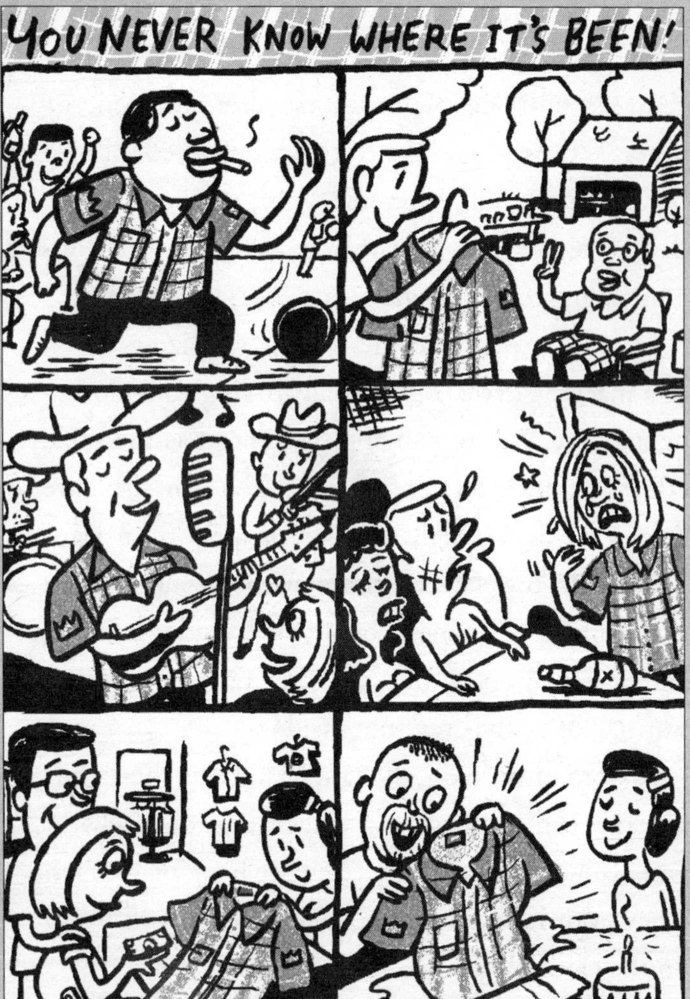
YOU NEVER KNOW WHERE IT'S BEEN!

Scoring on
the Down Low

CAN A PERSON get by on thriftiness alone? One member of the Mission Collective can almost make the claim, having procured 90 percent of his clothes, electronics, and furniture by shopping at secondhand stores.

Thrift stores are a fantastic resource for finding almost anything, and finding it on the cheap. This may seem like another no-brainer, but since amazing stuff can still be found at dirt-cheap prices, it seems like demand for secondhand is still lower than it should be.

For many people, thrifting has become a pastime. Many urban bohemians have even developed a fashion out of thrift-store finds. This is primarily because it's so much less expensive than buying new—even in San Francisco, where dirt-cheap is almost as expensive as Omaha retail. Generally speaking, you can save anywhere from 30 to 80 percent by buying used rather than new. Think of it as three or four pairs of jeans for the price of one!

While saving loot and looking good are the immediate consequences of thrifting, the ozone layer can benefit, too. Every time something is recycled in the market, energy is saved. Less packaging is used, less CO_2 is expelled into the air, and fewer resources are required.

If you're still not convinced, make a trip to a thrift store today and try to leave without buying something cheap, cool, and recycled. And trust us, after a few trips, the satisfaction of scoring that exceptionally unique deal will make all your hours of searching pay off.

Here are some online sources to find thrift stores near you.

Goodwill: www.goodwill.org

Salvation Army: www.salvationarmyusa.org

St. Vincent de Paul: www.svdpusa.org

The Shock and Awe of Paint

If watching paint dry doesn't fire any neurons, try these paint facts. Ever heard of VOCs, otherwise known as volatile organic compounds? That's the nasty stuff in oil paint that can cause indoor air pollution and ground-level ozone, even after the paint is dry. Stimulated yet? Try titanium dioxide. It's a pigment used in paint production that reacts to sunlight, producing smog. Jumping up and down, yet? Did you know latex has fungicides, preservatives, and other agents to combat mildew and rust? Of course, all of this has resulted in federal government regulations. Of course, in our opinion, these regulations don't go far enough.

You may or may not be excited about such facts, but the otherwise environmentally numb Department of Defense was sure set off by paint. In the late 1990s, the DOD collaborated with Green Seal, an environmental organization that has developed its own standard for environmentally friendly paints. You see, they needed to paint the Aberdeen Proving Ground, a huge facility, but the old paint had the mother of all ozone problems in the area. Working with Green Seal, they sought to cut down on paint pollution.

You can, too. Buy Green Seal–certified paints and recycled paint. Often these paints are cheaper than other kinds, and they are easy to find, too. Even Sherwin-Williams has a line of Green Seal–certified paints.

Keep it in mind the next time you want to liven up your life and cut down on the ozone in your home.

Living Green in the Paper-Full Age

A memo generated on untold reams of paper in the 1970s heralded the Age of the Paperless Society. Only the contemporaneous American changeover to the metric system matched the folly of the "paperless office" concept. According to the American Forest and Paper Association, paper consumption has increased about 13 percent since 1970.

Let's face it, until alternatives are adopted (see Upcycling, p. 85), paper is here to stay. Of course, our use of paper has a great impact on the health of our forests and on our planet. One way to reduce that impact is to conserve printing paper at home and at the office by trying the following:

1. Keep two piles of paper near your printer. One is fresh paper for important, final printing. Another consists of paper already printed on one side. Use the blank side for printing drafts and unofficial documents.

2. You can also use the blank side of the printed paper for notes and scratch paper.

3. Try your own hand at the paperless office. Get in the habit of saving information on disk rather than printing everything.

4. Recycle all paper when it has lived a full and useful life.

Another way you can conserve paper is by buying recycled paper products—like the book in your hands. The next time you're browsing for a new read, be sure to seek out titles printed on recycled paper.

They're Off and Running . . . to Work

It's 8:00 A.M. on the streets of San Francisco. Market Street is already packed solid with gridlocked traffic. Well, almost. Swerving between the cars and buses, a group of bicyclists moves at full speed toward downtown. Practically in a race, the bicyclists strive to get ahead of each other in a contest that is part skill and part showmanship. It's what they call getting to work.

For many people, getting to work is more than time lost behind the wheel. It's exercise. Of course, it doesn't have to involve the intensity of the Market Street madness. But biking to work can be a time to reflect, such as on the quiet stretches within Seattle's urban trail system or along the shores of Oakland's Lake Merritt or on the fifty miles of off-street bike trails in Chicago.

Or it can just be pure exercise. The U.S. surgeon general recommends thirty minutes of brisk walking every day. That's about two miles for most healthy adults, which makes getting to work on foot a possibility for many city dwellers, especially if they already spend an hour at a commercial gym doing exactly the same thing. And the more you walk, the easier it becomes to walk more.

Your favorite cookies are sold a mile from your house? Hey, that's only half the distance you walk to work every morning. And it feels a lot less guilty when you've burned the calories in that cookie by the time you're home.

Hush Patrol

Listening to music at "number 11" on your volume control has its place, but your black metal may be someone else's show tunes, and vice versa. Noise pollution is insidious and pervasive today, and everything from car horns to leaf blowers to blasting upstairs TVs is part of the problem. Just ask New York City mayor Bloomberg, who recently cracked down on those incessant musical ice cream trucks. Ongoing noise pollution can cause sleeplessness, depression, high blood pressure—and even heart disease over time.

You can do a lot to improve the situation by being aware of the noise you produce and having the guts to speak up against excessively high volumes on stereos and TVs in public spaces such as banks, supermarkets, and airports. And, if you want to take guerrilla action, there's always TV-B-Gone, a hand-held device that will shut off most televisions from a distance (www.tvbgone.com). Preserving the sanctity of the aural landscape is akin to giving everyone the right to hear themselves think. It's time to take back the (relative) peace and quiet, saving the high volumes for those wonderful places where they belong.

Saving a Bunny, One Perfume at a Time

Okay ten-minute activists, this one's gonna hurt. Go into your bathroom, grab a can of hairspray, open your eyes wide, and spray the hairspray into them. Well, imagine doing so, at least. According to the British Union for the Abolition of Vivisection (BUAV), that's what happens to some of the 100 million animals experimented on around the world every year.

Many argue that testing animals to curb or prevent future suffering of animals and/or humans is worthwhile. The debate could fill several pages, so we'll target one area of animal testing that is clearly unnecessary: cosmetics. Using animals in order to perfect lipsticks, antiaging creams, or hair products is more than just the worst kind of vanity; it's just plain cruel.

The Netherlands, Belgium, and the United Kingdom have completely banned vivisection. In 2002, the European Union agreed to phase in an almost total ban on the sales of animal-tested cosmetics, and to ban all cosmetics-related animal testing. In the U.S., the FDA actually encourages animal testing, while not requiring it.

If you feel strongly about animals being harmed in order to develop cosmetic products, do your research. Not all companies' antivivisection claims are entirely true. Some simply buy their animal-tested ingredients from third parties.

A list of the good guys and bad guys in the cosmetics industry can be found on PETA's Caring Consumer Web site: www.caringconsumer.com/resources_companies.asp.

Thinking outside the Cubicle

IS IT A workspace or a living coffin? A second-rate private office or gray-carpeted pacifier? However you look at the ubiquitous office cubicle, it is a fact of life for those of us who spend half of our waking hours inside them. But to what end?

The concern here is not how this affects your work efficiency (the boss can worry about that) but rather how being sequestered into a soulless cubicle will negatively affect your otherwise sunny and bright disposition. Unfortunately, the cube effect can carry ramifications outside the workplace. Who wouldn't suffer depression or snap at strangers after spending eight or more hours a day in something designed for maximum spatial efficiency? Hasn't anyone in corporate heard of feng shui?

Luckily, even the most isolated employee can take action. First: plants always help. Just ask the Russian cosmonauts who took plants into space on their record-setting space flights to keep themselves happy. Houseplant varieties like bowstring hemp (*Sansevieria trifasciata*) can even thrive in artificial light.

Second, you can lure other lonely cubicle-dwellers to your vicinity by putting out a jar of candy or fruit.

Your popularity will also benefit. Finally, decorate the "walls" of your cubicle with photos of good times, close friends, and serene settings. And remember, every photo of Yosemite Falls and every picture of your puppy equals its surface area in liberation.

Upcycling

The United States is awash in a stockpile of deadly chemical weapons, deployed to exact maximum effect on office workers, retirement homes, playgrounds, and toy stores. An Al Qaeda plot? Nope. Try a failed industrial paradigm.

Startling studies by Dr. Frederica Perera of Columbia University are uncovering how industrial toxins found in everyday life are accumulating in our bodies. Preliminary findings show that these chemicals (from such sources as cars, carpets, furniture, and jungle gyms) are increasing our risk of cancer and are being incorporated into our children's genes.

Does this mean modern life is incompatible with our health? No, say William McDonough and Michael Braungart. Both men are redesigning industry to enhance the environment, not poison it. But are these guys smoking too much grass? Actually, they're planting it on rooftops, such as at the corporate campus of clothing retailer Gap.

Imagine factories that produce no toxic waste because they use only materials that can be easily broken down by nature. Or imagine trash that is intentionally designed to degrade into compost for plants or can be remolded through biological processes into new products. McDonough and Braungart call such technology *cradle to cradle:* where products are designed to be at least as useful after their first use as on that first use.

And it's not a biodegradable pipe dream. Major corporations such as Ford Motor Company, Nike, and Frito Lay have used cradle-to-cradle engineering in factories and office complexes. Using so-called intelligent materials pooling, such companies are creating new, fully bio-degradable materials for their products. At the same time, they are redesigning their factories to use less energy and produce only biologically useful waste. An entire cradle-to-cradle community based on these principles is in development in Southern China, where homes and factories actually benefit the local environment. And new cradle-to-cradle products are coming out all the time.

Take a few minutes today to learn about what is available at McDonough and Braungart's Web site: www.mbdc.com. Or pick up their synthetic-fiber book, *Cradle to Cradle*.

Plant a Tree, Cut Down Costs

Picture a city in the blazing sun with no trees and a lot of pavement. Standing on the blacktop is like being surrounded by heated rock—as in a sauna. Okay, now plant a bunch of trees that shade all the roofs, parking lots, and streets. You would then be able to walk barefoot and be okay. Plus, since trees *create* a breeze, you'd be refreshed by the cooler blowing air around you. In the tree-filled city, fewer people need AC. Those are some seriously reduced emissions.

A "heat island" is a zone that's hotter than the rest of the land around it, usually due to lack of vegetation. With trees, the costs of cooling can drop by 40 percent. That's because trees are natural insulators, moderating the air temperature within their vicinity. Every time we cut down trees, we jack up our heating and cooling bills. Conversely, if we plant a tree, we cut down our energy use. And, of course, if you run your AC, there's a power plant puffing out CO_2—which trees can absorb.

Trees also filter our air, shade our kids from UV rays, raise property values, attract birds, and just make life better in general. Take a moment today to plant a tree. You can plant a tree in your yard or join a local tree-planting group. Check out the National Urban and Community Forestry Advisory Council for more information at www.treelink.org.

Spidey to the Rescue!

IT DOESN'T TAKE a rocket scientist to know there's something wrong with the air, but it did take one to discover a solution—Dr. Bill Wolverton of NASA, to be exact. And now you can execute that solution in your own home . . . and make a new, green friend.

Your home may be your castle, but it can also be your poison gas chamber. In newer structures, walls, furniture, and sealants are out-gassing nasty stuff like benzene, trichloroethylene, and formaldehyde. These gases cause rashes, allergies, and even cancer.

Hit the nursery or drugstore and buy yourself a shade-loving houseplant. The effort you expend will be nothing compared with that of your new flora companion who will filter out many gases (not tobacco smoke or dust, alas) in just a few hours. A single spider plant can absorb 85 percent of a room's formaldehyde in just six hours! And plants help keep your house cool, reducing the need for air conditioning.

Here's a short list of plants to consider:

Dwarf banana plants
Golden pathos (*Scindapsus aureus*)
Chinese evergreens

Peace lilies

Peperomia

Mother-in-law's tongue (*Sansevieria*)

Nephthytis (*Sungonium podophyllum*)

Popular indoor ferns (*Nephrolepsis*)

Pygmy date palm (*Phoenix roebelenii*)

Bamboo palm (*Chamaedorea*)

Spider plants (*Chlorophytum elatum*)

The Wicked *P* of the Elements

Ever seen a green lake? It may be the color of environmentalism, but a green lake is an unhealthy lake. In many cases, green lakes are a sign of phosphate pollution.

Phosphates are naturally occurring chemical compounds found in rocks. These compounds contain phosphorus, the P on the periodic table of elements. As water runs through rocks it collects phosphates, which are nutrients required by animals, human beings, and plants.

Phosphates become a problem when they enter waterways in excessive amounts; this usually results from human sources like farming or consumer products. Once in the water, excess phosphates endanger waterways, marshes, and lakes, usually by boosting algae growth. This, in turn, chokes bodies of water of oxygen, killing fish and water plants.

Even though many companies have stopped using phosphates, the average American still contributes three pounds per year of phosphate to the environment.

You can make a difference today. Two major phosphate-rich products you can avoid are fertilizers and laundry detergents. Many phosphate-free alternatives are available. For avid gardeners who must use fertilizer, you can use organic fertilizer rather than super-strength chemical fertilizer. Phosphate is the second number in the set of three numbers (the NPK percentage formula) located on the front of most fertilizer containers.

Using a commercial car wash can also help keep phosphates in soap from getting into storm drains (See Workin' It at the Car Wash, p. 214).

Keep your life green, but not your lakes: purge the P from your home.

People's History 101

If you're unfamiliar with Howard Zinn or his writings, don't feel bad. There are reasons why his kind of thinking doesn't make it through the commercial textbook pipeline. But this exclusion from the classroom doesn't mean his perspective isn't important, or even necessary.

Howard Zinn is one of the United States' most audacious historians, if only because he writes from the perspective of the everyday person, rather than from that of the presidents and generals. The good Doctor Z began a lifelong pursuit for peace and understanding while serving as a bombardier in

World War II. Later, in the fifties and sixties, he became an outspoken proponent of the civil rights movement while teaching at an all-black women's college. Zinn has also protested wars from Vietnam to Iraq.

Author of over twenty books, Howard Zinn's most famous and essential volume is *A People's History of the United States*. Telling the story of America from the perspective of its exploited immigrants, laborers, Native Americans, and slaves, *A People's History* is a fresh and honest portrayal of America's ongoing struggle to realize its ideals of freedom and liberty for all. Simultaneously, it is a heartbreaking reminder of how liberty is often crushed by corruption, classism, and prejudice. But it is also the story of real heroes, people who recognized their place in history and took action.

Every lifelong activist (and ten-minute activist) will find inspiration in Doctor Z's pages. Pick up a copy today, or visit Howard Zinn's Web site: www.howardzinn.org.

The Aggressive Tree-Hugger

If a tree falls in the forest, does anyone hear it? If so, the sound would be deafening. Across the world, forests are falling at unsustainable rates, and many of our major wood suppliers and retailers are betting that we don't care.

Luckily, the Forest Stewardship Council has provided the common wood lover with a way to let the lumber industry know we do, in fact, care. By purchasing wood that meets the FSC's Smart-Wood standards for sustainability, we can all have our wood without giving Mother Nature a mohawk.

Unfortunately, SmartWood is not is available in all areas. And often, big purchasers such as governments don't even know about SmartWood. So it's always a good idea to spread the word. Tell your local government you want your taxes purchasing only SmartWood. Talk to small wood and furniture stores or local shops about SmartWood. And before you stop at one of them call the Big Three wood purchasers:

Home Depot	(800) 553-3199
Lowe's	(800) 445-6937
Ikea	(800) 434-IKEA

Tell them that from now on, you won't spend a dime if you can't find the exact item you want in SmartWood. Don't let them snow you. They might stock some certified tropical hardwoods, but that's a *small* part of the market. Until we can easily get a SmartWood-certified two-by-four, we're barely making a dent.

Of course, the best forests are those that never get

cut down. Next time you want a new piece of furniture or other wood product, consider a used piece instead.

Backpackers for Bonobos

As you read this, another beautiful, wild species will have vanished from the universe for all time. Welcome to the Earth's greatest mass extinction ever, where one species of plant or animal disappears every twenty minutes—estimated to be between 100 and 1,000 times greater than any of the planet's previous diebacks.

You can throw your donations at the World Wildlife Fund or the Rainforest Action Network . . . money well spent, by the way . . . but there is an equally gratifying (and exciting) way to help save our fellow earthlings. It's called ecotourism.

More than just a safari, ecotourism is all about protecting animals and plants by giving governments monetary incentives to preserve their biodiversity. It also protects traditional people whose ways of life often depend on endangered ecosystems.

One of the darlings of the ecotourist movement is Costa Rica, which swapped debt for nature. Today, 28 percent of the country is a nature preserve, attracting tourist dollars from around the world. And there are many other options. You can ecotour to see pandas in China, rhinos in Nepal, or tortoises in the Galapagos.

In 2002, the United Nations Environmental Programme promoted the International Year of Ecotourism to build awareness of ecotourism's potential. As a result, over fifty countries developed ecotourist projects. But remember, not all ecotourism is equal. Many countries have abused the concept, so buyer beware. True ecotourism should be low-impact and sustainable and direct much of the proceeds to the indigenous community around the preserves. Happy trails . . . and tails.

Won't You Be My Neighbor?

They can be just a few feet from your pillow, their clamor disturbing your beauty sleep. Where do they scurry to during the day? You're pretty sure they have an active sex life. They're the enigmatic people next door.

It's a commonly held belief that neighborliness has suffered under the atomization of modern life. Casual evening talk in the town square has been replaced by coarse discourse via the Internet or boob tube.

Locked up inside, we seldom find the time to connect with the people next door. In fact, studies by Carnegie Mellon University suggest that time in the electronic environment increases people's chances of suffering from depression.

Take the time to create a neighborhood. When you move in to a new home, bake something for your neighbors. There's also the old "borrowing sugar" routine, but you could also try offering to share something you already own (see Share and Share Alike, p. 191). You could also try a little passive surveillance to discover what you have in common with your neighbors. Then contact them and bring up that interest. If you already know your neighbors, cement that relationship by inviting them to dinner.

Neighborliness not only helps us to be happier people, it can come in handy when problems arise. After all, it's a lot easier to talk about a problem if you already have a relationship established. Go get 'em, neighbor.

Giving a Helping Hula

We already discussed buying stuff at thrift stores (See Scoring on the Down Low, p. 71). Now here's the flip side. You can also save something by donating to secondhand stores. And not only will you help people in need, you'll assist in the global war against global warming.

Let's start with the money-saving angle. By donating your unwanted, underused, or outgrown items to a nonprofit, you're entitled to itemize these donations as deductions on next year's taxes. That's some easy green for just giving away yesteryear's hi-fi or that Halloween hula skirt.

Now, how does hula help fight global warming? It only does if that skirt dances its way into reuse. Every item sent to the landfill or incinerator takes time, money, and energy to process. Sending it on to a new owner means that unique item will live a little longer. And you might even launch the career of the next grass-skirt quartet in your area.

Check your phone book for thrift stores, homeless shelters, or your favorite charity next time you feel the urge to purge. And don't forget the receipt for the tax man!

Revisionist
Mind Control

IN MARCH 1989, poor Exxon got some bad press. It seemed that a certain oil tanker called the *Exxon Valdez* had spilled somewhere around eleven billion gallons of oil into the pristine waters off Alaska. Coming to their rescue, a covert group of advertising insurgents altered signs in California to broadcast Exxon's defense. The result: in San Francisco, a billboard for a local radio station was commandeered and its message changed from HITS HAPPEN, to SHIT HAPPENS—EXXON.

The Billboard Liberation Front has been altering and "improving" advertisements since 1977, when it did a face job on a Max Factor ad. Ever since, the shadowy cadre of marketing revisionists has lent their talents to various corporations and causes—all unsolicited and free of charge. How charitable of them. From big tobacco to the 2004 George Bush campaign, the BLF has taken the art of advertising to new heights—and new depths. Not only have they managed to put the art back into advertising, they've inserted a few facts, too.

Whether for inspiration or for some laughs, check out their online presence at www.billboardliberation.com.

An Order of Soup and Salad, and Hold the Malathion

Let's play the blame game. Who's the biggest contributor to water pollution in the United States? (a) urban and suburban neighborhoods, (b) farms, or (c) industrial plants? The answer: (b) farms.

Much farm pollution comes from the use of synthetic pesticides and chemical fertilizers used on food crops. Many of these substances have been linked to cancer and weakened immune systems. And they expect you to eat that stuff? Luckily, you have a choice.

Since April 2002, the U.S. Department of Agriculture's organic labeling rules have been fully in effect—a simple and clear system for certifying organic foods. You can see their rules at the USDA Web site. But the short and sweet on organic goes like this: organic vegetables and meat are defined in the United States as products grown without synthetic fertilizers, pesticides, hormones, or antibiotics. In addition, the U.S. organic label means the food is also ionization free and bioengineered free. Only foods made of 95 percent or more organic ingredients can display the USDA Organic label. And watch out! The use of the word "natural" is only 100 percent marketing. It has nothing to do with being organic.

Of course, organic food seems more expensive, but that's because the true social costs of commercial food are not priced in at your supermarket. Give your rivers, lakes, local farm workers, and yourself a break. Eat an organic meal today.

The Good, the Bad and the *Kinda* Ugly

When you flush the toilet, you don't usually think (insert echoing movie voice here) "Gosh, water is such a *finite* resource . . ." More likely, you're thinking you need to eat more salad. But, of course, water *is* finite. Worldwide, water demand is set to increase 40 percent by 2024. And no matter what, water will remain a limited resource.

Most towns designate water as "black" or "white." "Good" white water is piped into your house. "Bad" black water leaves as sewage. Within this black and white system, we waste a lot of "gray" water. Take the water you've used once, like laundry or dishwashing water. It's kind of ugly, but not too contaminated to be reused.

We should all encourage our cities to develop gray-water systems like the city of San Jose, California, has done; they collect and redistribute gray water. In the meantime, you can start your own at home today—no permit needed. In the kitchen, start with some quality biodegradable soap. Then use a basin to wash and rinse your dishes. Or, set up a valve under your sink to collect dishwashing water.

Then reuse the water for flushing your toilet—just dump it into the bowl when needed, and voilà! You've probably saved five gallons of water. You can also use about half a gallon of gray water per square foot per week in the garden. Where allowed, more intrepid conservationists can collect rainwater by installing a water catchment system on their house.

Unionize Your Tips

IN THE MIDST of the Roaring '90s, despite general increases in wages, nearly a third of Americans worked for $8 or less. That same year, a worker would have to earn an average of $8.89 per hour to afford a one-bedroom apartment. Since then, things have gotten a lot worse. According to the Economic Policy Institute, median-income families have seen their incomes decrease. Only 43 percent of American workers now have a pension. About the same number have health insurance. And those are the averages. If you look at specific groups like single moms or minorities, the picture is much grimmer. Meanwhile, those at the top have seen their incomes skyrocket over the past twenty years.

These numbers add up to real trouble for the working poor. They are the folks who serve food, work in elderly care facilities and clean houses and offices: we're talking about 6.4 million people.

So what can you do? Next time you're out for dinner, or calling in for a delivery, or get your car washed, unionize your tips. That service worker and his or her family is most likely struggling, often only a paycheck or injury away from homelessness. Take your tipping off autopilot and buffer the usual 15 percent tipping rate with a little social awareness. Try 20 percent or even higher. Go for an extra dollar at the coffee shop or bar. And don't be dissuaded if that corporate eatery or café doesn't allow a tip jar. Veto their corporate ethos and tip 'em anyway!

Unbranding Your Ass

If the revolution were only a T-shirt away, we might find that it's already been trademarked. Like most things in life, apparel has been transformed from something comfortable, warm, and even handsome, into an advertisement for sweatshop-owning corporations.

Even if you're not aesthetically displeased with being branded like a cow, with a company name emblazoned across your chest, you might still have reservations about how that article of clothing was made. If so, you'd share that sentiment with Naomi

Klein, author of *No Logo*, a much-celebrated book of the antiglobalization movement.

Complaining that fashion was turning us into walking billboards, Klein's book splashed onto the international scene within weeks of the infamous antiglobalization "Battle in Seattle." That event woke the public up to the problems of free trade, and Klein quickly assumed a leading role in communicating dissent. Ever since, she has published works on human rights and social responsibility that have appeared in numerous publications.

Take a minute or two to catch up with Klein at her Web site, www.nologo.com. Then, remove the stink of the sweatshop from your own clothes by removing the company names that advertise them.

Weekend Warriors

Occasionally, ten-minute activists have to put in some overtime as weekend warriors in the name of street protests. Public protest is about as American as you can get, since there would be no America without the protests of the 1770s. Unfortunately, someone forgot to tell the authorities.

As activists, it's important to know your rights, as well as your strengths and your vulnerabilities. To begin, the U.S. Constitution guarantees the right to protest on public property. You can protest without a permit on any public sidewalk if you remain out of the street and obey traffic signals. Protests in parks and in the streets, or demonstrations using amplified sound, usually require a permit. Protests on private property require the owner's consent.

Political meetings are also protected, but are sometimes infiltrated by police on fishing expeditions, or worse. Undercover police *never* have to reveal themselves, and can actually break laws in order to protect their cover.

If you're marching and get caught up in police action, it's important to be safe. When confronted by angry police, it can be helpful to use de-escalation techniques, like raising your hands up, making no sudden moves, and assuring the police you're not a threat. In case the police use tear gas, bring along a squirt bottle to wash your face and eyes. Synthetic water-resistant clothing can help protect your skin.

Finally, if you're arrested, use group solidarity. Jails and courts are ill-equipped to deal with organized groups. You can use that power to win concessions.

More information can be found at www.law collective.org.

Don't Be a Pusher for Your Bovine Buddies

The "official" word is that the synthetic bovine growth hormone rBGH, injected into cows to increase milk production, is perfectly safe. Yet while the FDA approved agribusiness monster Monsanto's little darling, it's interesting that Canada and Europe turned it down, and the Cancer Prevention Coalition and Oregon's Physicians for Social Responsibility are just a few of the many organizations strongly discouraging its use. Why? Because the artificial hormone creates an insulinlike growth factor that could be linked to premature growth in infants and young children and the increased risk of breast and colon cancer in adults.

And let's face it: rBGH is just not nice to cows. It turns them into stressed-out milk-producing machines, shortening their lives and subjecting them to chronic mastitis, resulting in more antibiotics and even pus in your milk.

The best bet for those who indulge is to request and buy milk products with an rBGH-free label. Even better, look for organic milk produced by independent small farms where cows can actually frolic, eat real grass, and feel the sun on their backs. Think about the role cow's milk has played in building your bones ever since you were a wee thing. For all they've done for us, it's the least we can do for them.

Warm-up Act

On a cold day you come home, rush over to the thermostat, and just crank that baby up. You're freezing and want to get warm quick. The hotter you set the thermostat, the quicker you'll get warm, right?

If only life were that simple. Fact is, your thermostat doesn't work like a gas pedal. Turning it up higher won't make your room heat up any faster than pushing an elevator button harder or faster will make the elevator move quicker (though some try it anyway). The thermostat simply turns the heater on and off at the temperature you set. In fact, temperature increase is actually decided by how much heat your heater can throw off.

It's also important to remember that heat is a fair-weather friend. It's easily lured outside by cold air. If you want it to stick around, you'll have to lock it inside with you.

The average home has air leakage equal in size to a three-foot-square window. That's ample opportunity for hot air to escape. A little weather seal on the windows and doors can save anywhere between 5 and 30 percent a year on your heating bills. For those without the time or hardware budget, just plop a few blankets under doors and windows in the drafty rooms.

In the meantime, while waiting for the heater, go the low-tech route: drink some tea.

The Energy Star
on Your Block

IF WASTED ENERGY made a sound, your inefficient clothes washer might sound like a leaky balloon. But your refrigerator ... the one built in 1985 ... that would sound like a freight train derailing in your kitchen. According to the California Energy Commission, that old fridge costs you 60 percent more energy than one built today. And if you choose an energy-efficient model, you could save much more. Talk about cold, hard cash!

The U.S. government, for once, has made it easy to save energy. Check out their Energy Star program (www.energystar.gov), which lists energy-efficient products from refrigerators to dishwashers to furnaces. You'll save big bucks on energy costs *and* you'll reduce your household's contributions to global warming. After all, our home energy use can create twice the greenhouse gases driving a car.

Once you've replaced your old appliances (and disposed of them properly), you can make your house a lean, green, domestic machine and be the envy of all your big-energy-bill neighbors. That sizes up to pretty big bragging rights at the next barbecue.

Voting for Lemon Meringue

What do you get if you mix one part Bill Gates with one part free-market guru Milton Friedman and one part former WTO head Renato Ruggiero? A pie in the face, that's what.

More humane than its progenitor, tar and feathering, pieing is a delicious way to wipe the smirk off the face of authority with a soft lather of coconut cream. The pie's comedic roots began with Keystone Kops and the Marx Brothers, but took on a political flavor in the 1970s. Activist Aron Kay is considered the first political pie thrower for having pied Anita Bryant, a homophobic activist and singer.

Since then, the torch of cream liberation has been passed on. Belgian anarchist Noël Godin and the loosely organized Biotic Baking Brigade are notable examples. As Texan rascal Jim Hightower once said, "Pies are the Boston Tea Party of our modern day." That's because pieing is mostly harmless (although an ego or two has been crushed in the process) but has such theatrical power that it can draw quick attention to any issue.

You can join the food fight with nothing more than a disguise, a cream pie, and a worthy target. Remember, the softer the throw, the safer for everyone. The point is not to hurt, but to humble. Happy landings!

Ditch the Dash-and-Trash

When you're running late to work, and just keyed up for that big ol' jelly donut (Elvis style!), a cup o' java sure hits the spot. The quick fix for coffee consumers on the go is often the ditch-and-dash solution: a throwaway cup. But there's no reason to let your morning ritual become a global garbage epidemic.

Starbucks calculates that one paper cup per day equals an entire tree per year! And according to the Circle of Life Foundation, using a real cup has the following *positive* impacts:

- Energy use is reduced by 98 percent.
- Water pollution is reduced by 99 percent.
- Air particulates are reduced by 86 percent.
- Greenhouse gases are reduced by 29 percent.
- Solid waste is reduced by 86 percent.

Multiply all this by a few friends, and that adds up fast. But select your coffee cups carefully. Plastic mugs (especially when exposed to heat) have been shown to give off xenoestrogens, which are known to cause cancer. Instead, stick to metal or ceramic mugs.

However you manage it, most cafés try to do right when you bring your own cup by giving you back the money they save on cup costs. Others might need a little education, though you might want to wait until after you've had that first cup!

The Dark Side
of Bleach

IT'S TRUE: good guys don't always wear white. But when they do, the really good ones steer clear of bleach.

Chlorine bleach (aka sodium hypochlorite) can be dangerously toxic to you and your environment, and can even be fatal if mixed with certain other common household cleaners. In fact, every year thousands of injuries result from chlorine bleach having been mixed with ammonia or acids (usually found in toilet cleaners). Each of these in combination with chlorine bleach chemically reacts to cause a highly toxic gas. No joke. Be mindful of what you're using next time you clean your kitchen or bathroom.

As if that wasn't enough, the chlorine bleach that leaves our drains can be especially toxic to our marine ecosystems—it depends on the level of treatment your local sewage system uses to remove the chlorine bleach toxins before they reach our lakes and oceans. You can call your local utility or just err on the side of safety by not using bleach as a rule.

As far as laundry goes, it truly is an old wives' tale

that bleach is the best way to whiten your whites. You just don't need advanced chemistry to get whites white. Check your local shop for alternatives to bleach using environmentally neutral ingredients such as hydrogen peroxide or sodium percarbonate. Or, try our "green" whitening alternative below.

Bleach alternative: Add lemon juice to some water, then pour it into the wash along with two tablespoons of borax.

Peace Paper

The Japanese gods have a rule: you can have whatever you want if you just fold 1,000 origami peace cranes first. They made that rule because they hate all our squabbling and know that even with all the wealth in the world, none of us will be truly happy until we've ended war.

Millions of children across the world have taken

the Japanese gods up on their offer. Every year, they send bushels of colorful folded cranes to Hiroshima, inspired by the story of Sadako, an eleven-year-old Japanese girl who died of leukemia in 1955. Sadako was two years old when the world's first atomic weapon was used on human beings. She, too, had taken the gods up on their offer, hoping that, through peace, no more children would die from wars as she did.

Of course, origami can be for simple pleasure too. But if you value peace, do it for humanity as well. You can place your peace crane next to the thousands of others below Sadako's monument in Hiroshima's Peace Park. Or you can send it to the warmonger in your family. Or send it to your national leader. Or just put it into your window, as needed.

To learn how to fold origami cranes or to read Sadako's story, visit www.sadako.org.

Peace.

Gleaning for Goodness' Sake

When you reap your harvest in your field and forget a sheaf in the field, you shall not go back to get it; it shall be left for the alien, the orphan, and the widow . . .

Deuteronomy 24:19 (NRSV)

The above biblical quote illustrates that "gleaning" is a practice that goes *way* back. Traditional gleaning was basically setting aside crops left over in the fields after the harvest for the needy. Obviously, this is still relevant in some parts of the world, but assuming the only apple around your house is a laptop, it's probably not the most likely way you'll glean (though everyone should try the traditional method sometime).

Today, the practice is probably better referred to as "food redistribution" or "food recovery." Even the most self-indulgent among us can glean food that would otherwise be wasted. You can glean from the restaurant, from the caterers, or from the super-market. All it takes is collecting it and putting it into the hands of people in need. Here's an outline of modern ways to glean:

- Collect perishable produce from wholesale and retail sources.
- Collect prepared foods from the food-service industry.
- Collect processed foods with long shelf lives.

After the collecting has been done, get the food to a homeless shelter or soup kitchen, or give it directly to anyone obviously in need of a meal. You'll be the angel of your neighborhood . . . at least for a day.

Comfy Conservation

In 1979, Jimmy Carter did the unthinkable. He dressed like Mr. Rogers. Carter's famous cardigan-clad energy speech occurred amidst the OPEC oil crunch. Determining that the United States' national security was at stake, Carter outlined a conservation plan that included such cutting-edge technology as placing wool sweaters over our T-shirts in wintertime.

But you don't have to just wear a sweater to save energy. You can start with the way thermal energy is transferred around your home. In the kitchen, you can take advantage of residual heat. Turn off your heater when you plan to use the oven. And remember, just after you turn off the stove burner, your frying pan is still hot enough to keep cooking. Use that lag time to save energy by turning burners off a little early.

You can also use the residual heat of your morning shower. Time your heater to go on a little later in the morning and take advantage of that piping hot water. You'll be hot enough when you get out, so a fully heated house is counterproductive. By the time you've cooled down, your house will be warming up.

Residual heat might seem like nitpicking. But a difference of one degree Fahrenheit in your house can reduce your energy consumption and greenhouse contributions by 5 percent. Make a few of your own observations about your life patterns to discover tailor-made ways to cut down on energy costs.

Guerrilla Gardening

Back in the 1970s, sunflowers became the symbol of the German Green movement, partly because Germany was ground zero in the cold war and sunflower seeds were known to help the body process radiation more quickly. Now they're an international symbol for renewal and reclamation, and their little yellow faces do a nice job in dressing up almost any shabby corner of the landscape.

Is there a crack house on your block? Chemical waste treatment plant? Pee-stained alley? Neutralize the bad vibes by planting the seeds an inch deep, six inches apart, in the spring. A native of North America, sunflowers grow well in most climates as long as they're planted after the last frost and have access to full sun. They'll attract birds in the summer and produce new seeds in the fall, and almost any variety will do—except roasted and salted. So while it's sadly true that we can't all live in Pee Wee's playhouse, we can still perk up the neighborhood with a little Technicolor vegetation for the people.

Big Brother v. the Little Guy

"A paranoid is someone who knows a little of what's going on."

—William Burroughs

Big Brother and his corporate touts are watching you. They know your shopping habits, the kinds of books you buy on Amazon.com, and the kinds of movies you watch via Netflix. They've put spyware on your music CDs and have built databases to track who you call. Had enough? But there's more. They've also tracked your movements via your cell phone. And, they trade your personal information for their own profit and at your expense across international boundaries.

How do we know all this? Because the Electronic Frontier Foundation is monitoring the monitors. The EFF was founded in 1990 and has fought for consumer digital rights, privacy, and free speech ever since. Currently, they're the guys suing AT&T on your behalf for handing over your phone records to the National Security Agency.

Over the years, the EFF forced Sony BMG to stop including spyware on music CDs, spyware that created security vulnerabilities on our computers; overcome a Justice Department attempt to stop citizens from using identity protection software on their computers; and forced electronic ballot companies like Diebold to make public the source code of their machines used in our elections—in addition to stopping them from holding secret meetings with government officials.

Make today the day you acquaint yourself with their latest efforts and learn about the current incursions into your life at www.eff.org.

Slaves
for Chocolate

LET'S BE HONEST about three things: we love chocolate, slavery is horrific, and we shouldn't have to wonder if we're supporting slavery by eating an ordinary chocolate bar. But the fact is, we probably are. Today significant numbers of children in impoverished areas of Africa (an estimated two hundred thousand in Ivory Coast alone) are kidnapped or otherwise forced to work against their will on cocoa farms, where they are frequently beaten and starved. Not a very sweet situation.

Since Ivory Coast grows 40 to 50 percent of the world's cocoa and the beans are sold in mixed lots by brokers, the odds are good that a slave had a hand in producing most of the standard chocolate of unlabeled origin consumed throughout the world. The safest bet right now is fair trade chocolate, since fair trade certification guarantees that independent farmers get a fair price for their crops, eliminating the main cause of slavery.

And since most chocolate products include the company's phone number on their packaging, why not give them a call and tell them how you feel about their cover-up? You can start with Hershey's at (800) 468-1714. If little schoolchildren were able to stop the needless slaughter of dolphins for tuna production, then supercharged chocolate lovers can surely unite in halting one of the most heinous human rights violations on earth. Here's to guilt-free indulgence, at last.

Know Your Dealer

He hangs out on the street corner. His hands are always a little grimy from the dirty business of his trade. You probably recognize him from his hushed bywords: "Fill 'er up?" He's your neighborhood dealer.

Like all dealers, oil companies come in many shapes and sizes, but in the end, we usually get played. Lately, a few of these companies, like Shell and British Petroleum (BP), have promised us they've changed their ways. No more executing environmentalists in Nigeria or spilling oil in Alaska, we're told. They're going clean and green.

BP is now marketing itself as Beyond Petroleum. To prove it, they invested millions into green technologies like biofuels and solar energy. And Shell has invested in wind power and finally admitted global warming is real.

But both companies continue to relapse: spilling

oil, illegally flaring gas from oil wells, making arrangements with dictatorships, encroaching on tribal lands. The list goes on.

So how's a ten-minute activist to respond?

It may be too early to tell how sincere the green dealers are, but the alternative energy investments are real. Meanwhile, all the other pushers, from Exxon on down, are behaving as badly as ever.

Of course, our primary goal should be to wean ourselves off oil. But in the interim, we should keep an eye on these guys and see if we can't form a support group together. It could be through consumer power that we could nudge them into being totally straight and solar.

Air Supply

The American pika, a small stem- and clover-eating, mountain-dwelling relative of the rabbit, is rapidly disappearing thanks to the destruction of its food supply through global warming. If you drive a car, you can help the pika and save over a hundred dollars a year by simply keeping your tires inflated to their maximum pressure. Here's how, in five easy steps:

1. Buy a tire pressure gauge. A good one will run you around $15, and it's also a great tool to swap and share.
2. Consult your car's owner's manual for the highest recommended pressure or psi (pounds per square inch).
3. Take a quick reading every few times you go to the pump. Make sure to take the reading at "air temperature," not when the tires are nearly frozen or steaming from the heat.
4. Inflate as necessary.
5. Cash in with better mileage.

Keep in mind that your car will handle differently as the tire pressure changes, so don't engage in any *Dukes of Hazard* stunts until you're used to the new equilibrium. If everyone did this, we'd save four million gallons of gas a year, reducing emissions and sparing the atmosphere for everyone, including the innocent pika. An added bonus is less wear and tear on tires and a built-in tire-safety check for the lazy.

Here's to the upside of inflation!

Yo, Ho, Ho and a Cheap Radio

U.S. law says that the airwaves belong to the people. And yet, ten corporations control two-thirds of the U.S. radio market. The result is what we have today: a coast-to-coast, lowest-common-denominator, broadcasting desert. But swashbuckling against these stale DJs and tired formats comes a merry band of pirate broadcasters.

Pirate radio is broadcasting that isn't licensed by G-men. Instead, it asserts the public's right to broadcast without permission. There have been pirates on FM, AM, shortwave, and even television, all giving communities their own on-air personalities.

Pirates live by three rules: (1) don't step on other broadcasters, even the big guys; (2) since mainstream broadcasters have bailed on the community, serving your area is crucial; (3) don't be a jerk—corporate radio has enough of those.

It's not a crime to buy and sell broadcast equipment. But it is to broadcast with it, for most people. The feds take a dim view of liberated airwaves. Historically, though, they've messed with just a few, mostly high-profile, long-term, or foolish pirates.

Pirate radio is cheap and easy. Pirates can get set up for a few hundred dollars. An FM station would need only an RF amplifier, a compressor/limiter, an antenna, a microphone, a cheapo audio mixer, and a boom box or MP3 player. In general, 100 watts of pirate power is plenty. Of course, there's always online broadcasting or podcasting for shoestring pirates.

For more info, see: members.tripod.com/~transmitters or www.dxing.com/pirate.htm. Welcome aboard, matey!

Put Your Money Where Your Mind Is

WHO SAYS PLAYING the stock market has to be bad for the planet? Look beyond the Enrons and Exxons of the world to a greener, and, yes, more profitable market. Socially Responsible Investing (SRI) is growing across the investment world, making up 8 percent of the current professionally handled investment capital. And it's often more profitable than traditional portfolios. According to Peter Camejo, green veteran and author of *The SRI Advantage,* socially-minded investments do better because companies with an awareness of their responsibilities to society and to the environment often avoid business decisions that result in class-action suits and similar liabilities.

Show you the money? Take the Ariel Fund (ARGFX), which screens its holdings with socially responsible criteria. Over the past ten years, it has consistently outperformed the S&P. There are also funds that focus on particular progressive technologies, such as the WilderHill Solar and Wind Power Fund (PRB) that goes up as oil grows more scarce. That's a sure bet if there ever was one.

There are dozens of individual stocks for green companies involved in energy-conserving technologies and green consumer products, as well. So if you're investing your money, take a few moments today and look up an SRI broker in your area at www.progressive-asset.com. And if you don't invest, turn an investor friend on to SRIs.

Land of the Lost

It has an annual budget of $35 billion and employs over half a million full-time employees, making it larger than any Fortune 500 company except GM. Its economic and political power makes it an irresistible lobby that almost always gets its way. Meet the United States prison-industrial complex.

Understanding the scope of the U.S. incarceration crisis requires perspective. In China, with its infamous detentions of journalists and religious dissidents, there are an estimated 300,000 prisoners. The United States, with a fifth of China's population, has 2 *million* prisoners. That's 25 percent of all the prisoners in the world.

Whether U.S. prisoners are generated by racism

(58 percent are black), runaway poverty or the epidemic of drug abuse, their plight is everyone's plight. Overcrowded and secretive, U.S. prisons have become incubators of HIV, hepatitis C, and violence. One in four women prisoners is raped, often by male guards. Prisoners are sometimes isolated in solitary confinement for months or even years. Human rights abuses such as refusing medical assistance and racial taunts by guards are rampant. And more and more, teenagers are imprisoned alongside adults.

There are two simple actions one can take. Start with educating yourself by becoming a prisoner's pen pal. One route is www.prisonpenpals.net. Don't be put off by ads for sexual relationships. Many also seek platonic correspondents. However, be sure to use common sense when giving out personal information. And use a P.O. box as a return address.

Prisoners also need books. You can donate books or even phone directories to prison libraries. The people on the other side will appreciate it.

Takeout for the World

Here's another true but revelatory scenario: a boyfriend is asked to pick up an order of takeout from a Vietnamese restaurant for himself and his girlfriend. When he shows up, the cashier ushers him back to the kitchen and hands him something resembling an oversized Crock-Pot. A little confused, the boyfriend accepts the pot and proceeds to his girlfriend's apartment across the street. As it turns out, the pot belongs to his girlfriend. Since she often frequents the restaurant, she hates wasting the cardboard, plastic utensils, and other disposable products, and so supplies the pot herself. Another ingenious individual in action!

While it may not always be practical or convenient, it doesn't take much effort to reduce the amount of unnecessary materials that will go to waste when taking out your dinner. Here are some other approaches to eco-friendly take-out:

- Never accept unnecessary plastic utensils, condiments, paper or plastic bags. Instead, use your own utensils. Lacquered chopsticks are easily wiped clean for reuse and can be carried anywhere. Or, recycle the plastic utensils for next time.

- Bring your own bag from home. You might want to tell the staff person that you will do so when placing your order so they don't bag it before you arrive.

- Finally, establish a relationship with the restaurant staff. Most likely, they will be more than happy to accommodate you as it will save them money on packing materials as well as help to reduce waste.

Erotic Recycling

It's the digital age. Whether you're rocking out to good vibrations or getting off on good vibrations, battery power equals pleasure power. And as our fun becomes more gizmo-centric, the demand for batteries to power up will increase, as well. In fact, an estimated 4.7 billion batteries were used in 2006; the number goes up 6 percent a year. That's mondo fun, but also a megamess.

Studies have shown that only about half a percent of all batteries are recycled after they are used. That means a mountain of recyclable metal and plastic is going to waste. More significantly, batteries contain hazardous metals that pollute the environment and unnecessarily take up a good deal of landfill space.

Luckily, states such as California and New Jersey have brought this problem to the public's attention by making it illegal to simply throw away batteries. There are easy and simple steps you can take to keep out of trouble. Many national drugstores, hardware stores, and electronics chains are now required to accept your used batteries with the responsibility to recycle them. Some cities are also providing public recycling bins designed for consumers to have easy access to enviro-friendly recycling for all kinds of batteries. You can recycle batteries from cell phones, electronics, computers, and yes, even vibrating ears of corn.

To find a recycling center in your neighborhood, simply go to www.rbrc.org.

Kill Your Junk Mail

Impersonal, wasteful, presumptuous, time-consuming, environmentally degrading . . . the list goes on. Not even the loneliest of us looks forward to a mailbox full of junk mail. But if you don't already hate it enough, check out the stats.

Eighty million trees are wasted every year in this mail-driven, hopelessly desperate drift-netting for your dollars: that's about a tree per household! And in case you're wondering, that amounts to about $450 billion just to transport and dispose of this marketing clutter every year. In fact, it's been estimated that the average American wastes eight months of his or her life dealing with it. Thank you, Madison Avenue.

So since we all agree that we hate junk mail, how do we kill it? Start at its source. The biggest culprit is the Direct Marketing Association (DMA). The DMA is the Mac Daddy of the ad pimps that sell your contact information to junk mail advertisers. There are several other companies, though. You can contact them all through a form letter made available at www.ecocycle.org/junkmail.

Another tactic: when signing up for a credit card, buying a magazine subscription, or joining an organization, always mention that you don't want your name or address shared with other companies. To stop the current blizzard of credit card solicitations that beat on your indebted door, you can call (800) 5OPT-OUT. You can also go to your local post office and ask to fill out Form 1500. It's a legally soundproof way to reduce unwanted mailings.

Bulk Bin Binging

BULKING UP AT the grocery store is all about lightening up . . . on packaging, that is. Bulk food is gaining traction across the land. Even major supermarket chains have begun installing a few bulk item bins. The fact is, people just like it. Whether you're a chocolate-covered-raisin connoisseur or a bulk-black-bean binger, you get to buy the amount you want, at lower cost, and without all the packaging.

For the math-minded reader out there, here are some numbers to chew on. Packaging accounts for half of all paper produced in North America, 90 percent of all glass, and 11 percent of all aluminum. And, all told, almost a third of the waste generated in the United States is packaging.

Shopping in bulk is an effortless (bulk-food grazers would say fun) way to have an impact on the packaging problem. You'll save landfill space and a significant amount of natural resources.

Better bulk food sellers carry many items in bulk. You can find everything from oil to flour to pasta. Sometimes you can even find instant soup stock, exotic teas, and no-frills fig bars.

It's likely there's a bulk food store near your house. But if not, don't be shy about letting your local store know that you desire a bulk food selection. Give them the market rationale: you want to save money and intend on shopping where bulk food is available. And remind them that wholesale bulk foods cost stores less as well.

Boss Your City's Money

No matter where you live, you pay local taxes. Some is sales tax or property tax (if you rent, your rent pays the tax). And some taxes are tacked on to your utility bills. And then there are hotel room taxes, fuel taxes, and parking fines.

All that cash goes somewhere. Some gets spent on stuff like parks and potholes, and some gets invested. And in each case, someone decides where the dough will flow. Will it go for more bike lanes, or for more parking? What about a needle exchange, or a great recycling program? These are important questions, and (since you obviously read important books), you should have a say.

Crashing the local budget party isn't that hard. In lots of towns, you can get on a finance committee just by stepping up. There just aren't that many people who get involved, which leaves a lot of spots open.

To start, make a list of the top five things you'd like your town to fund, and the top five things you'd not like it to fund. When you're done, call city hall and talk to the people who make the decisions— usually the finance director, controller, or treasurer— or just talk to the staff who put the budget together. Tell them your name, what you want, and why. And tell them that you'll be checking back with them.

Remember, you paid your taxes, too. That makes you entitled to be the boss of how the money is spent.

Know Your Rights

In the United States, the right to remain silent is the right most often heard. It's repeated a thousand times a week on TV, in movies, and in children's games. Sometimes it even comes up in politics. Also well known are the rights to free speech, to religion, and to a free press, among others in the U.S. Bill of Rights. But did you know you have the right to view art? How about the right to employment and just pay? Or the right to an education?

It's true. Such rights are clearly spelled out in a document signed by the United States: the Universal Declaration of Human Rights, ratified by the UN General Assembly in 1948. The declaration consists of thirty articles listing rights that apply (in principle) to everyone on Earth. So if you are, in fact, a citizen of planet Earth, this document covers you.

While not legally binding, the UN document is constantly used by lawyers, parliaments, and supreme courts. That's something called precedent, and it weighs heavily in courtrooms.

There are too many rights to list here, but they are available online. As a whole, they show our species to be quite advanced, despite recent evidence to the contrary. The document is written in simple language and takes less than five minutes to read. So go ahead. Check out the UN's Web site at www.un.org to know your rights, earthling.

Will Trade Puppies for Pearls

A carefully detailed painting measuring 2.5 x 3.5 inches just sold for . . . another carefully detailed painting measuring 2.5 x 3.5 inches. Welcome to the world of artist trading cards, a bartering system where artists create miniature art to trade with other artists. Commonly traded through online services like eBay, trading small artwork actually goes back centuries, just like bartering.

Bartering is a means of exchange in which no cash is used. Instead, the participants exchange goods and services for other goods and services. In Los Altos, California, it's plants. Every year, plant lovers gather at the town's Garden Club to barter seedlings and plants. On the Internet's Craigslist, people exchange boats for bikes, laptops for lumber, or maid services for music lessons.

Unlike when we pass money across a cash register, bartering almost always generates conversation—and gets to the heart of what it is to be a human being. This is especially true when the items being exchanged are things we made, or things we used. There's always a good story or two that gets traded with each item. So, while the dollar may still be king, bartering is the joker in his court, always good for livening up humdrum commerce.

Take a look around your house today and see what kind of item you could barter.

Take a Trip on the Wild Side

The couple making out in aisle 11 just met. In six more hours they won't even sit together. The guy next to you is fiddling with his pocketknife. He won't look you in the eye at the rest stops. That's how it is on the Dog, otherwise known as Greyhound Bus Lines.

If you like your coffee weak, your stories long-winded, and your fellow passengers out of a David Lynch movie, and you want to reduce your greenhouse gas emissions while traveling, you'll love the adventure served up diner-fresh aboard every Greyhound bus. Often for less than the admission to the circus!

Of course, the Dog is not the only animal on the road. There's also the Green Tortoise, for a crunchier ride. Partly fueled by patchouli fumes, the Green Tortoise bus line runs from Alaska to the Yucatan. Best of all, you can stretch out on their bunks while traveling at night and arrive refreshed at your destination in the morning.

For those partial to more grandeur, more space, and better toilets, there's nothing like train travel.

Still chugging around the bend, trains continue to roll throughout North America. Not bound by the interstate, you can sit back with a drink in the café car and watch the road-free scenery pass by. Or, play cards with your fellow passengers.

Whether by train or bus, getting there is half the fun. For your next vacation, garage the car and join the party.

The Lot
of Hot Air

WHEN ENGINEERS DESIGN electrical circuits and devices, they try to make sure their gizmos give off no heat. Why? Because heat indicates poor performance—

wasted energy. That's right—making heat with electricity is, by definition, inefficient.

That makes electric space heaters just about the most colossal waste of energy out there. They're actually *designed* to waste electricity through the use of lame circuitry. If you want a real treat, take a look at your electric meter and see how much faster it spins when there's a space heater turned on.

Many space heaters have a figure like "1,500 watts" printed on them. Do the math: it's like lighting fifteen 100-watt bulbs, or twenty-five 60-watt bulbs—*all at the same time*!

Sometimes landlords give or recommend electric space heaters to their tenants because they don't want to put in gas lines or radiators. That often means the tenant gets stuck with the enormous heating bill. Let your landlord know you want a more reasonable (nonelectric) heat source. You won't believe the money you'll save, even if your rent goes up.

If you have the choice and don't already have one of these pieces of junk, don't buy one—ever. And tell your friends and family not to use them. If you have one, get rid of it. Don't even give someone else the chance to use it. You'll save yourself and them crazy money—and lots of power.

Good-bye Kitty

This book is full of grim statistics, but the following may be the worst of them all. In the time it takes you to do a ten minute action, seventy-five cats and dogs will be killed in animal shelters. That adds up to four million a year. Nobody dislikes this practice more than the people who work for the shelters, but with limited resources and few takers, the animal atrocity goes on.

Each euthanized animal is a fury bundle of love that would warm any heart . . . and lap. Fact is—pets help us stay healthy and happy. But they also require care and money. Too often, people take on pets without considering the work involved. As a result, millions are abandoned or given up to shelters.

There are lots of actions we can take to remedy this situation. If you plan to add a pet to your family, consider all the costs and responsibilities involved first. Then, choose your pet from a shelter and not a pet store, many of which produce animals in puppy and kitty mills that only add to the overpopulation problem. Even young animals and purebreds can be found in shelters. If you must have a hard-to-find breed, do a little research to find a humane breeder.

Fostering abandoned dogs and cats is another action you can take. Shelters also need volunteers to walk dogs and play with cats, which is a great way to have animal time if you live in an apartment that doesn't allow pets.

Got Heart?

Giving to others is probably the most basic form of charity. Saving a life is charity's greatest act.

Incredibly, there is a way that you can do both, simultaneously, at no financial cost.

Nearly 100,000 U.S. citizens are currently awaiting an organ from a donor. On average, eighteen people die awaiting a transplant every day. It only takes a few minutes of your time to secure a chance at several more years of life for someone awaiting a new liver, kidney, heart, or other vital organ.

We are all potential donors. Your age and health status will not necessarily preclude you from helping someone who needs a new organ. The cost to potential organ donors is nothing outside of the few minutes and ink it requires to fill out a form. After deciding to become a donor, be sure to notify your family of your decision to avoid any potential legal snags. And you can rest assured that your donation will not be capriciously awarded to the next Dick Cheney on the list. Income and status play no role in prioritizing organ recipients.

The laws and rules for becoming a donor vary slightly from state to state. In some, you can sign up as a donor when applying for a driver's license. www.shareyourlife.org has all the necessary information on becoming a donor for each state.

Blinding the Watchers

The eye is upon you. If you're in China, it might be Yahoo. The Western Internet company has reportedly given records to Chinese authorities that led to the imprisonment of journalists. Here in the West, we have our own kind of all-seeing eye. It sits in secret rooms at our phone companies or in front of computer screens in corporate marketing departments. Day and night, it monitors our Web activity.

So what to do about it? Get tech-savvy, that's what!

Luckily, this is easier than ever, thanks to spirited work done by programmers across the world.

www.peacefire.org makes available its Circumventor tool to allow Chinese Internet users to access Web sites censored by Beijing. Tor is another. Tor is proxy software made available through the Electronic Frontier Foundation (see Big Brother v. the Little Guy p. 135). Tor is like a spear in the all-seeing eye, making your online browsing much more private. Tor works by providing a private network for users. This network is made possible by volunteers who donate their bandwidth. When you install Tor, you are able to join this volunteer network.

Unfortunately, the Tor community is growing faster than its numbers of volunteers, which means that when you use Tor, your Web browsing will be slower. One fix for this uses a Tor button plug-in available for some browsers. This makes it possible to turn Tor on and off with a single click, so you can blind the watchers when privacy is more important than speed.

Tor is available at: www.tor.eff.org.

Bookworms of the World, Unite!

"Freedom itself is a dangerous way of life, but it is ours."

—The American Library Association

BY DAY, THEY sit modestly behind reference desks and checkout counters. By night, they fight overreaching government agents and work to shrink the digital divide. Who are they? They are your local librarians.

Highly misrepresented as hush-happy fuddy-duddies, librarians are actually outspoken, cutting-edge, social activists dedicated to preserving freedom of speech, privacy rights, and digital rights. They have been in the forefront of the debate over the USA Patriot Act, the fight against government secrecy, and finding a balance between copyright protection and consumers' fair use rights.

You can meet these heroes and heroines of information freedom by visiting your local library. Like all superheroes, they're always available to help the public. And what you find in their fortresses of freedom might even surprise you.

Today's libraries have more than just dusty books on improving your checkers game on their shelves. Many libraries have extensive music and movie collections available for you to take home and enjoy. Some libraries also double as community meeting spaces, lecture halls, cinemas, and art galleries. And some are works of art in themselves. San Jose's King Library in California, for example, incorporates thirty-three artworks by artist Mel Chin into its building, including rolling tables that fit together like jigsaw pieces and glass vaults of "banned" books hidden under certain book stacks.

Visit your local library today to see what your local library activists are up to.

Green Printing

Anyone with a computer printer, a copier, or a fax is faced with two choices. Be green and prosper, or be a stooge for oil companies. Simple, right? Except that every year, millions of people choose oil.

According to Citizen Campaign for the Environment, 350 million printer cartridges are dumped or incinerated every year. Since it takes a gallon of oil to produce one printer cartridge, that's a lot of money invested in oil companies and clutter in our landfills.

The green alternative is even the *cheaper* alternative. Many cartridge retailers will now trade used cartridges for a free ream of paper or refill your old cartridge with fresh ink at a reduced cost. Or, you can buy a refilling kit for next to nothing and refill your way to oil independence. Meanwhile, you'll save nearly 70 percent on buying cartridges. That translates to guilt-free, pollution-free printing.

Green and Clean

Sure, your medicine cabinet has a box of Band-Aids and some pain relief medication, but do you have an aloe plant? If you burn or cut yourself, that prickly plant could be a warm fuzzy (or should we say, a cool soothey). Just slice off an arm from the aloe plant (*Aloe vera*) and wipe the oil that oozes out onto your wound. Studies show the plant's gel speeds up the healing process.

Aloe is literally a green home remedy, and there are dozens of others out there. And they can do more than just heal our bodies. They can heal the environment. Consider that in 2004, 850 billion gallons of domestic pollution washed down American drains. That's more pollution than industry created. Below are a few green remedies to reduce your own household's impact.

GREEN REMEDY	INGREDIENTS
Wood floor cleaner	1 gal. warm water mixed with 1/4 cup vinegar
Nonwood floor cleaner	1 gal. warm water with a drop of mild detergent
Surface cleaner spray	Lemon juice in water
Abrasive cleaner	Bicarbonate of soda with a wet cloth
Window cleaner	Vinegar mixed with water
Carpet cleaner	Sprinkle bicarbonate of soda on stain, vacuum
Dish cleaner	Pure soap and water

Toilet cleaner	Warm soapy water
Clothes detergent	Pure soap and baking soda
Facial wash	Plain yogurt (feels so good!)

Free Word

Read an earth-shattering, life-altering book lately? Maybe it was Tim Flannery's *The Weather Makers* or Eric Darton's *Free City*. This time, instead of displaying it prominently on your shelf with all the other literary statements, why don't you release it back into the wild where it can work its magic on more people?

In the past, literary activists would just leave their books in public places such as cafés or on train seats. But what happened next? Did the book get picked up by a backpacker en route to Tierra del Fuego? Did it shatter destructive illusions instilled in a child's mind? Happily, there's now an organization that can reveal the secret world of recycled books.

Established by Ron Hornbaker in 2001, www.bookcrossing.com will register your book and give you an ID number. Then, once the book is "tagged" with instructions for the next owner, you can plant your literary gem anywhere and track its progress as each successive finder posts comments and reactions to the book on the Web site. With over 450,000 members worldwide and three million books currently registered in the catch and release program, it's a kinder, more literate way to spread the word about important causes—and also have the thrill of tracking your book.

Of course, for those who want something simpler, there's still community charity donation or the old-fashioned fateful leave-the-book-on-the-sidewalk plan. One thing's for sure: someone will pick it up.

Compost Happens

RECYCLING ORGANIC MATTER requires energy. However. the human energy required is practically zero. In fact, we expand more energy taking kitchen waste from our house to the dumpsite. Now consider how valuable that organic material is. It took a lot of energy to create those banana peels and egg shells.

When dumped at the landfill, all that energy potential is lost. Worms, beetles, and centipedes are the work-horses that make compost happen, but you don't have to be intimate with them to compost. Below is a simple method to turn garbage into organic fertilizer that is clean and odorless, and avoids the bugs.

This method has two stages: an indoor and out-door stage. For indoors, you need two five-gallon buckets with lids. One bucket is for holding *untreated* sawdust, obtainable for free at lumber stores. The second bucket is for layering kitchen waste. To get started, put two tablespoons of charcoal or a layer of grass clippings on the bottom of the second bucket to combat odors. Next, add a thin layer of sawdust, then your kitchen waste (no meat!), followed by another layer of sawdust. Keep layering sawdust and vegetable matter. When it's full, take it outside.

The outside stage can vary. You can dig holes to bury your compost, but this method slows the com-posting process. Faster composting requires heat, so build a compost pen of untreated wood or chicken wire in the sun. The compost is ready for use when it breaks down into dark matter.

Vroom Vroom Goes Buzz Buzz

There's a holy war going on, and you're right in the middle of it. On the one side, you've got an e-angel urging you to get an electric vehicle (EV). On the other side, a devil wearing a GM T-shirt is telling you that's impossible: the auto companies already shredded the prototypes. However, EV technology is not only straightforward, it's increasingly affordable. So, if the film *Who Killed the Electric Car?* doesn't resurrect EVs, growing consumer demand just might.

EVs can recharge overnight and can have a range of up to 320 miles. With fewer than 10 percent of the moving parts of a regular car, no oil changes, and no tune-ups, maintenance costs are dramatically reduced. The best deal about EVs, though, is their efficiency. If you were to convert their power into gasoline equivalents, an EV would get 110 miles per gallon!

While much of their electricity is generated by fossil fuel–powered utilities, EVs pollute less. That's because power plant electricity is 90 percent cleaner than the exhaust from an automobile.

There are options aplenty when going electric. Many companies, such as California's AC Propulsion and Canadian Electric Vehicles, sell EV kits to convert cars to electric for $8,000-$10,000. If you own a hybrid, like a Prius, you can easily convert it to a Plug-in Hybrid Electric Vehicle (PHEV) and drive thirty miles on pure electric power every day. Hymotion of Canada is planning to produce PHEV kits for Priuses for $9,500 by 2007.

More information is available at the Electric Auto Association at www.eaaev.org.

Go Wild

With ocean fisheries under intense stress (see The Ocean on the Ropes p. 9), you might naturally conclude that farmed fish would be the way out. After all, we replaced hunting with domesticated animals, right?

Unfortunately, there's something fishy about current fish farming practices. Most of the fish we eat are carnivorous. On the farm, they're fed pellets of ground fish. But those pellets actually concentrate the pollution that fish accumulate in their bodies. Many wild species, such as swordfish and king mackerel, are known to be too toxic to eat now, but the problem is much worse in farmed fish, which can have ten times the PCBs in their meat as wild fish. There's also concern over the use of untested drugs in farmed fish.

Farmed shrimp are especially bad because shrimp farms have damaged mangrove swamps, polluted the ocean, and contaminated surrounding farmlands. They've also been responsible for outbreaks of marine diseases in ocean areas.

Sadly, the contamination of the Earth's water systems means that even wild fish are no longer reliably safe to eat, especially for pregnant women and children. However, if you gotta have your fish and chips, go wild when you do.

Most wild-caught fish are labeled. But as with any fish story, there's still a "catch." The FDA doesn't regulate fish labeling, and *Consumer Reports* discovered, almost half the salmon labeled "wild" were actually from farms. That means we need FDA rules, as for chicken and beef. Until that happens, buy carefully, from trusted sources only.

Pooling Resources

From the time we're born, we're always looking for another shot at being weightless and wet. Pools are great fun and fantastic exercise, especially for people with injuries. But pools and spas are a major downer when it comes to energy and freshwater usage. Heating water is one of the biggest energy drains in our homes, so imagine heating ten thousand gallons a day!

If you're the lucky duck with the pool or spa on

your block, be sure to follow a few energy-saving tips. Get a well-fitted cover to save up to 50 to 70 percent on heating costs. There are also solar covers, which save even more energy. Plus, pool covers reduce water and chemical evaporation. If you rent, badger your landlord to use a pool cover.

Also ask a pool technician about the minimum number of hours your pool's automatic pool sweeping and filtering equipment needs to run. Then set the equipment to run only as much as needed. You can also save energy by doing annual checks of the equipment, including checking the thermostat and de-liming the heat exchanger.

If you're planning on installing a new pool, consider a skin-loving saltwater pool. They don't require adding dangerous and expensive chemicals because the chlorine is produced from the salt in the water.

Finally, share the wealth. Pools are excellent things to share with your neighbors (see Share and Share Alike, p. 191.)

Share and
Share Alike

IN ATLANTA, GEORGIA, people are walking off with hundred-dollar tools without paying, and the guys behind the counter couldn't be happier. Welcome to

Atlanta's ToolBank Tool Lending Library. Every morning, a line of trucks pulls up and are soon filled with everything from shovels and routers to sawhorses and band saws. All you need is a library card and they're yours.

Sharing has gone rather out of fashion these days, but it's still an age-old tradition that makes sense. Even if your library isn't as hip as Atlanta's, we've all purchased expensive items that could be shared. In many cities, people have begun sharing cars through organizations like zipcar.com and citycarshare.org. On craigslist.org, they're trading vacation houses and sharing rides.

Individuals can also share their big items with neighbors. Put up a list of loanable items you'd be willing to make available in your apartment building or condo complex, or around your block. Or talk to co-workers about ways the employees can share outside of work. Items you might consider sharing could include kitchen tools, camping equipment, cookout equipment—or how about that supersucker vacuum all your neighbors envy?

The Great White in the Kitchen

If there were an appliance food chain, the refrigerator would be at the very top. Think of your fridge as the great white shark of energy-eating appliances. And just as sharks are always swimming, refrigerators are always *running*. If either one stops, they die . . . and begin to smell.

But whether you own your own fridge or one is furnished with your apartment or house, there are several easy steps you can take to increase your fridge's efficiency, combat global warming, and save some money.

The first step is recognizing that one fridge is enough. That underused second one in your basement or garage is responsible for a big chunk of your power bill and, like all fridges sold in the United States, releases global-warming hydrochloroflourocarbons

(HCFCs). Also, look for energy-efficient models bearing the Energy Star label when shopping for a new fridge. And if you still think you need two, one large one is much more efficient (that is, cheaper) than two medium-sized fridges.

Finally, maintain the fridge correctly. It should be kept at 37–40 degrees Fahrenheit. Any colder than that is simply a waste of energy. Freezers should be kept at 5 degrees Fahrenheit. Also, check for an "energy saver" switch and turn it on. And, from time to time, clean your fridge's condenser coils (the metal loops located on the back or underside that make your fridge cold). Dust them twice a year to ensure that your shark is swimming healthfully and not dragging you under.

Caution: CrimethInc. in Progress

To think is not wrong.
Just don't think wrong, citizen.
Buy this? Bad idea.

What better way to start talking about *thoughtcrime* than a haiku? Vague, secretive, lean, and infectious, thoughtcrimes are ideas we're told not to have. Says who? Says the thought police, of course. Ever questioned authority? Stupid question. Thought something was odd about laugh tracks? Think again. Those are exactly the thoughts you must scrub clean, right?

If you don't buy the "better safe than sorry" warnings of the thought police, help is out there. Fittingly, the solution is more a school of thought than a group. It's called CrimethInc.

CrimethInc. holds that our minds are jailed in the cells of politics, religion, and economics—not always the most honest institutions out there. So, CrimethInc. finds tools to help us always think freshly and freely, and reminds us that the world is far more than we've dared to think it could be.

CrimethInc. puts out books, Web sites, makes videos, supports musicians, and does a whole lot more.

Sometimes you can tell it's CrimethInc. Sometimes you can't. Look for CrimethInc. at a supermarket near you. And if it's not there, help the supermarket stock up. Visit www.crimethinc.com.

Paper or Plastic?

It's the moral dilemma of our age, striking every time we reach the grocer's checkout counter: "Paper or plastic?"

Both paper and plastic bags take energy to produce and destroy. Plastic bags are made from non-biodegradable polyethylene and take thousands of years to decompose. When not disposed of or saved properly, they become ugly urban tumbleweed, blown around until eventually catching on our car wheels or sticking to a rosebush. It's been estimated that in New York City alone, if each person used one less plastic bag a year, it would eliminate five million pounds of waste and save

$250,000 in disposal costs each year. Just one bag per person!

On the other hand, unrecycled *paper* bags take up huge amounts of landfill space that could be used for other, more necessary waste. Plus, they are made from beautiful trees.

The correct answer to the paper-or-plastic quandary is really a no-brainer. It's neither. Simply invest in reusable cloth or canvas tote bags. Many stores now sell them and in fact offer discounts for either using your own bag or reusing bags from previous shopping trips. Reusing your old plastic or paper bags is okay, but eventually they will break or rip and need to be thrown out. Canvas bags, however, will last for years and are more aesthetically pleasing. Simply keep a couple in the car or around the house and bring 'em with you on shopping day. Case closed.

Power Plants

IT MIGHT SOUND corny, but corn power is for real. So is switchgrass power and sugar power. No, this isn't some new energy-packed breakfast cereal. It's biofuel.

For billions of years, plants have converted sunlight to energy, depositing some of it as fossil fuels in the form of coal and oil. But it isn't necessary to wait eons for plants to create energy. Current technology makes it possible to harvest biofuel from plants after one year's time. The bonus with biofuels is that, unlike oil and coal, when you burn them, you're releasing last year's CO_2—reabsorbed by this year's biofuel crops.

So-called biofuels are not the wave of the future. They're the wave of right now. Brazil is the global leader, with 80 percent of new Brazilian cars running on domestically produced ethanol, made from sugarcane. Americans can get biofuels, too. That little socialist-engine-that-could, Berkeley, California, has beat the rest of the United States at the capitalist supply-and-demand game through vegetable oil-based biodiesel. Free classes are held at the Berkeley Farmers' Market every month by the Berkeley Biodiesel Cooperative to teach the public how to make and use biodiesel for their cars. In San Francisco, you can buy biodiesel for $3.50 per gallon. That's just a little more than gas, but without all the wars and oil spills.

Best of all, with biofuel, you're in the driver's seat. Biodiesel can often be made right in your own kitchen. Talk about energy independence!

Tranquil-o-Motion

Nowadays, movement can be murder. Everyone has seen that passive-aggressive road warrior who has to sniff everyone's bumper but then refuses to pass when given the opportunity. Or how about that cell phone user who leaps from one near miss to another, oblivious to it all. And we can't forget the bicyclist cutting off pedestrians on the sidewalk.

Clearly, for some people, their vehicle is an extension of their bad attitude. So why not make your car or bike an extension of your positive attitude? If you live in an area with tolls, try paying the toll for the person behind you. When others are merging into your lane, don't just let one person in, let two or three. When stopped at a light on your bike, make eye contact with the drivers nearby and give them a big, happy smile. It's not hard to imagine the effects of such simple but extraordinary acts of generosity. It's even possible that your kindness will rub off—just like all the bad voodoo so clearly does.

Happy trails!

Runaway Bag Escapes Poop Scoop

Once upon a time, you were walking down your street and a plastic bag caught on your leg. Your first thought was to condemn the culprit who had just tossed it on the ground, littering your neighborhood. You kicked it away and walked on, grumbling about litterbugs while assured you shared none of the blame.

But, oh! If that bag could tell you its story! The truth is, it started its journey to your leg the day before, a full mile from your block when its former owner, a green-leaning granny, carefully recycled it in the dog-poop dispenser at the park. Moments later, a dog pooped. When the dog owner pulled a bag out of the plastic bag dispenser, the green-leaning granny's plastic bag got loose. It was windy that day and the plastic bag filled like a sail and lifted above town, only to find your leg after a great journey.

Now, if you had been there when the dog pooped and were able to catch that bag before it flew off, wouldn't you have done something besides kick it away? Of course you would. Your proximity and understanding would have compelled you to do the right thing.

Next time you take that ten-minute walk, note the adventuresome trash lost on your street and take responsibility to ensure that their travels end in the recycle bin or trash. It might be a cigarette butt that gave its life for cancer. It might be a sheet of newsprint with its own runaway story. You can't be sure. But you can be courageous . . . and make the neighborhood a little prettier at the same time.

Smartmobbing the Man

What do Chinese nationalists in Shanghai have in common with outraged voters in Manhattan and Boston? Here's a hint. It's the same link that connects antimonarchists in the Persian Gulf to South Korean teenagers. Give up? It's smartmobbing!

Smartmobbing is the latest electronic tool used by protestors to outwit the man, whether he's the local security force or the national overlord. At the heart of smartmobbing is SMS, commonly known as text messaging on cell phones. SMS technology gives individuals up-to-the-minute information on political actions being planned, but can also help coordinate efforts during the often chaotic moments that occur at rallies. For example, smartmobbers can inform one another through their cell phones where help is needed, what intersections require bodies, or what the police are up to in a certain location.

If SMS is Greek to you, check out Howard Rheingold's book, *Smart Mobs: The Next Social Revolution.*

Be a twenty-first century Paul Revere by getting connected before the next big rally. More than a great way to stay up-to-date on what's going on, you'll add another body to the "mob" that's driving dictators, robber barons, and school principals into a corner.

Frankenfish Fillet

IMAGINE A LAKE polluted by heavy metals from a nearby factory. Now imagine a genetically engineered fish, designed to spend its life soaking up and storing those heavy metals, effectively cleaning the lake. Sounds good so far? Now imagine that toxic swimming storehouse is eaten by another fish—a trout. A day later, a fisherman catches that trout and brings it home for dinner.

Genetically modified organisms (GMOs) are plants and animals that have had their genetic structure tinkered with, creating corn that produces its own internal pesticide or rice that can produce plastic. While this might sound like science at its best, it could be disastrous, like the example above.

The Union of Concerned Scientists has listed a number of potential nightmare scenarios in which Frankenfoods and Frankencritters escape into the wild. Aside from the fish scenario, GMO plants might cross-pollinate with their wild cousins, creating super-weeds. Another concern is that plants engineered to produce Bt toxin in their tissue might allow insects to become immune to Bt toxin, one of humanity's greatest tool in fighting pests. Another is that fiddling with plant DNA might activate sleeper genes that pro-duce toxins and allergens when turned on.

Don't want Bt toxin in your cereal bowl? In the United States, the FDA does not require labeling of GMO products. So finding out what you're buying can be difficult. However, Greenpeace has compiled an online true food shopping list. Check it out at: www.truefoodnow.org/shoppersguide.

Eat, Drink, and Be Very . . . Slow

Feel dis-integrated? Is the speed of life going up and up for you? Too much bad food fueling your extended workday? Does the phrase "hand to mouth" generate rumblings in your gut? Luckily, there's an appetizing way out of the contemporary frenzy—at least temporarily. It's called Slow Food.

Slow Food is just like it sounds—the antidote to the causes and effects of our fast-food culture. It focuses on connecting us with what we eat, by building understanding from the plow to the plate and strengthening culinary bonds with family, friends, and communities. Most of all, it helps us slow down and take a moment to enjoy the foundation of life: food.

Slow Food International got its start in 1986 in Italy, when Carlo Petrini learned that a McDonald's was to open in Rome's historic Piazza di Spagna. He lost that battle, but ever since, Slow Food has grown (at a pace that's anything but slow) into a worldwide movement. Slow Food USA, for example, has programs and projects aimed at identifying and revitalizing food traditions that are at risk of extinction; educating schoolchildren about the values of eating locally, seasonally, and sustainably; and connecting a network of five thousand small-scale and sustainable food producers across 130 countries.

You can slow down with your local Slow Food convivium group. To find one in your area, or to start one up, go to www.slowfoodusa.org.

The Phantom Bloodsucker

It's broad daylight, but that's not stopping the vampires in your house. Got a microwave or VCR flashing the time? More than a visual annoyance, it's a bloodsucker. How about that glowing doorbell button? It's a round-the-clock bloodletting. Worse, many appliances and most computers give no clue that they're still sucking juice even after you've pushed the "off" button.

All of these are examples of what's called a "phantom load," but a vampire load is more like it, because they truly suck. In most U.S. homes, phantom loads are about 6 to 15 percent of all electricity used. Do the math: if your phantom load is 8.3 percent, that's a month's worth of electricity every year!

The main suckers are machines that:

- have a clock or glowing light
- have a remote control

- use a "wall wart" transformer (a power brick)
- are in some way connected to your computer

Try this vampire detection test: unplug every single thing in your house, including your fridge. Then look at your electric meter. The more juice you use, the faster that thing turns. If it's spinning, you still have something plugged in. Once it's not spinning, go back and plug in one machine at a time and check the meter again. If the meter spins, the vampire's back in action.

A power strip with its own on/off switch works like a stake in the vampire's heart. Use a strip for your machines. When you hit the strip's power button, the sucker is stopped dead. Happy hunting.

The Tissue Issue

Whether it's dealing with relentless allergies, providing comfort during a sad movie, or just basic bathroom hygiene, we all use heaps of tissue. But did you know that much of that wiping relies on ancient old-growth trees? Go ahead, ask that burning, incredulous question: Why would *anybody* use such rare and valuable lumber to make paper for our booties and boogies?

The answer: because old growth trees give us the ultrasoft yet strong tissue discerning butts, tear ducts, and nostrils have come to expect.

Kimberly-Clark is one of the top five wood buyers in the world, producing the very tissue we love so much. Greenpeace and the National Resources Defense Council have led a campaign to pressure Kimberly-Clark to halt their buying of old-growth wood, especially from the boreal forests of Canada. Environmentalists allege that only about one-fifth of Kimberly-Clark's products come from recycled materials. That's a good start, but we can do better. If every 175-sheet, virgin-fiber tissue box was replaced with 100 percent recycled paper, 163,000 trees would be saved.

The next time you stock up on tissue, make sure it's 100 percent recycled. There is no shortage of tissue and toilet paper made from recycled materials, but there *is* a shortage of old-growth forest.

Workin' It at the Car Wash

Shine up your roller skates and slip into your short-shorts, its car wash time!

Oh, but before you get all sudsy and excited, it's important to understand a few facts about washing your car. First, you shouldn't wash your car at home. That's right, roll up your hose, pack your disco, and move it on down to the *commercial* car wash.

Car washing at home is just bad boogie. You'll probably use up 116 gallons of water and be your neighborhood's worst polluter for the day. When we wash our cars, we usually do so on pavement. That means all the exhaust buildup, petrochemical residue, heavy metals, and other nasty things coating the car wash straight into the storm drains, which lead right to wetlands and beaches.

Commercial car wash facilities, however, use about 60 percent of the water, reuse much of it at least once and then send the waste to the water treatment plant to make it safe. It's gonna cost you up front, but the otters, egrets, and shellfish will thank you.

Of course, many car washes also fund worthy causes. If you're washing cars to fund-raise, try to work out a deal with a commercial joint. But if you can't, wash on gravel or grass, which can help filter the residue. Also use biodegradable, phosphate-free soap. Plus, get a flow-restriction spray-gun attachment to more efficiently squirt your car—and your friends.

The Sudsy Truth

HERE'S A BRIGHT idea. Let's soak all the fish in the world in antibiotics and dioxins! Actually, they already have been, thanks in part to antibacterial soaps.

Nowadays, antibacterial soaps are everywhere, and we've been fed a line of bull saying we need them. In fact, it turns out that infants actually need germs around to create a good immune system.

Triclosan, an antimicrobial agent regulated by the U.S. Food and Drug Administration, is the usual ingredient in such soaps. When mixed with chlorine in tap water, it forms chloroform, a probable human carcinogen. And sunlight turns it into dioxin. Once down the drain, these toxins enter the water supply, showing up later in groundwater, streams, and, yes, fish—but also breast milk.

The senseless use of antibiotics could possibly foster resistant strains of bacteria. So right now, that antibiotic soap in your house could be generating burly superbugs rather than knocking them off.

Ready for the punch line? According to the American Medical Association, they don't even work better than regular soap! So chuck all that antibiotic soap and tell your grocer and friends why you did.

To *really* kill germs, wash with ordinary soap and warm water. Rub your hands together, making sure to wash your fingers well, and wash up past your wrists, for fifteen seconds—about the time it takes to sing one round of "Twinkle, Twinkle, Little Star."

Actionless Action

If you haven't heard, the day after Thanksgiving has been unofficially changed from "the busiest shopping day of the year" to Buy Nothing Day. You won't see any holiday advertising for it, but it thrives nonetheless. Buy Nothing Day has snowballed into a kind of anti-consumerist global holiday, prompting millions to save rather than spend and consider rather than consume.

How easy can activism get? All you have to do is boycott spending for a twenty-four-hour period. What does this accomplish? When millions of concerned citizens across the globe show their solidarity by refusing to shop, spend, or buy for an entire day, it helps others realize what a large and potentially powerful consumer base they are a part of. It also gives us time to consider the consequences of mass consumption on the environment and our well-being.

But there's no reason why your personal Buy Nothing Day has to be confined to one specific day of the year. That day is chosen for its obvious symbolic significance (in the United States at least). Try setting aside one day a month where you don't spend a dime. Eat from the back of your fridge or cabinets. Walk or bike to work if your car needs gas. Stay home and read a book instead of going out. Whatever it takes. You'll be amazed at how cleansing it feels. And if you're sold on it like the millions that love Buy Nothing Day, try an entire Buy Nothing Weekend.

Chillin' with My Farm Boy

Downtown Detroit: struggling inner city, home of record-setting murder rates, and a great place to get fresh corn so sweet you don't even need to cook it. Welcome to Detroit's Eastern Market, one of the country's growing number of farmers' markets.

City folks don't usually get ultra fresh vegetables, but thanks to the recent rebirth of farmers markets, local farmers are making it possible. According to the U.S. Department of Agriculture, there are more than 3,700 farmers' markets in the United States, twice the number from ten years ago. This is great news for everyone. Farmers' markets allow us to meet the people who grow our food, allow farmers to get feedback from their customers, and give us a great way to come together as communities. The food is usually fresher, too, and that means it's more nutritious. And best of all, the money you spend goes straight to the small independent farmer rather than to some agribusiness middleman or supermarket chain. Many markets also offer a chance for local craftspeople and musicians to introduce themselves to their neighbors.

It's true community at its traditional best. Check out the growing list of American farmers' markets to get in on the action at www.ams.usda.gov/farm ersmarkets.

The Endangered
Species Menu

WE ALL GET hot and bothered when we hear that the cuddly panda is endangered or when poachers bring down a herd of noble elephants. But few raise an eyebrow when the venerable shark gets his fin cut off for someone's trendy soup. But sharks, like pandas and elephants, are endangered, and their disappearance would be a blow to the ocean's health.

Sharks are one of the oldest species in the ocean, and many ecosystems, such as coral reefs, have evolved to depend on their role as the top predator. But this relationship is threatened by the growing popularity of shark meat in the West, coupled with rising incomes in the East. There's a good chance the fish in your "fish and chips" is shark, for example. That results in nearly 100 million sharks harvested each year.

At the same time, sharks are poisoned by pollution just like every other fish. That's where your own health can be at risk. Being at the top of the food chain, sharks accumulate the heavy metals and other toxins stored in their prey. In fact, they contain some of the highest concentrations of mercury in fish.

It's time to stop the feeding frenzy. The next time you see your favorite restaurant or fish market selling shark, let them know why it's a bad idea. Tell them honestly, or simply stop buying shark meat. Do it for your health and the ocean's health.

Lights, Camera . . . Take Action!

If there's a Michael Moore or a Morgan Spurlock in you, you might want to indulge your filmmaking dreams and bring your video camera to the next political rally you participate in. Video cameras are increasingly common sights at rallies. Whether it's documenting the street theater, the silly costumes, or just your own participation, the handheld video camera can also be an activist's best legal tool.

A legal observer is someone who photographs, logs, or videotapes police action at political rallies. He or she documents any arrests, police misconduct, and even civil rights abuses that may occur. Ever heard of Rodney King? That was video activism's first big media splash.

If you bring your camera to a rally, observe a few tips. Have a friend watch your back while you film. It's also handy to have a runner you can pass the camera off to if needed. There have been incidents where police have attempted to confiscate cameras at rallies or even arrest videographers. Though any charges will be dropped, you might lose your precious footage.

If you witness police violence, be sure you remain nonviolent, neutral, and let the police know that you're filming them. Often that reminds them that the civilized world is watching. Also be sure you write down any incidents you've witnessed as soon as possible, before you forget the important details.

You can get more video-activist tips from www.videoactivism.org. They also have online video sent in by other video activists that you can watch.

Green Laundry

The dirt on laundry isn't pretty. It uses a load of energy and needlessly adds pollutants to the environment. There's nothing clean about that. However, by tweaking our laundry-washing habits, we can save energy, lower our bills, and reduce pollution.

When washing laundry, use cold water whenever

possible. Using a cold rinse and a warm wash can save well over twice the energy as hot water for both cycles. We have suggested turning water heaters down to 120 degrees (see Give Me Shower or Give Me Death, p. 61). In fact, 120 degrees is hot enough to clean grease and deep dirt.

That takes care of the energy problem. What about laundry pollution?

The manufacturers of conventional detergent have stopped using phosphates in their detergents because many states have banned them. Yeah, democracy! But now detergent companies are using synthetic phosphates, which we know little about. Boo, loopholes!

Regardless, conventional detergents are manufactured from synthetic petrochemicals and synthetic surfactants. Few, if any, of the ingredients in conventional detergents biodegrade in a reasonable time frame, and they aren't necessary to clean clothes anyway. Fortunately, we have a choice. There are non-chlorine bleaches and detergents available with ingredients that biodegrade. It isn't difficult to find a list of readily available, eco-friendly detergents by looking on the Web or simply asking at your local store. Or, make your own detergent by checking out our suggested detergent recipe (see Green and Clean, p. 178).

Your Money *and* Your Life

Every time Americans "charge it," an Islamist martyr gets his wings. Osama bin Laden said so much when he outlined his strategy of bankrupting the United States through endless war in the Middle East. But we have more than Al Qaeda to blame for our debt woes. Thank Asian bankers, American politicians, credit card companies, and, yes, the American consumer.

If you normally don't pay attention to economics, you may be forced to soon. The International Monetary Fund is warning of a financial meltdown spurred by American borrowing. At every level, it looks bad.

The federal government's budget deficit was $25

billion in 2003, but is expected to mushroom to $783 billion by 2020. The U.S. current account deficit (the difference between what we import and export) hit 5 percent of GDP in 2003. That's the level economists call the tipping point—where an economy runs into serious trouble.

Over half of Americans have no savings and a third barely scrape by, and consumer debt is up 39 percent since 2000. Meanwhile, the credit industry is booming, and popular money gurus like Suze Orman are promoting "fabulous" credit card indebtedness to young people.

Scared straight yet?

Bad news aside, it's not too late for individuals to get their own house in order. Take Oprah's advice and put yourself on a "debt diet." Get rid of unnecessary credit cards and luxuries like cell phones, cable TV, high-speed Internet, or whatever else you can think of. And start saving for that rainy day. It may come tomorrow.

Clone Attack

IMAGINE TAKING A trip to your local video store to get that movie about a clone war. Now, upon arriving, you notice another video store across the street. That's not unusual. It's actually healthy to see some competition. But something's amiss: it's identical to the other video store: the name, the colors, the neon overkill. It's a clone!

The incredible duplicating chain store is multiplying everywhere. Often, the clone store is just a stone's throw from the first. The result: café, drugstore, and fast-food chains are monopolizing our public spaces and making clones of all our communities. In turn, clone stores limit our spending choices by driving out independently owned retailers.

There's a name for clone warfare. It's called "saturation strategy." The idea is to saturate an area with so much competition that mom-and-pop operations can't stay in business. As soon as the local shop goes, the clones consolidate, leaving behind empty warehouses, vast, unused parking lots, and wrecked local businesses. This is the strategy made famous by Wal-Mart. In fact, Wal-Mart made famous another strategy: assisting the de-industrialization of the U.S. by favoring products made in China.

If you don't like dead downtowns or dead-end economics, or you just can't stand the sight of so many clones, you're hardly alone. Hundreds of towns have won local battles in the clone war. You can see a list of victories against Wal-Mart at www.sprawlbusters.org. If you don't see your town, use the force and put it there!

Culture Jammer

Earnest, smart, and cute as an oompa-loompa, former ad agent Kalle Lasn decided to fight fire with fire in 1989 and formed *Adbusters,* a magazine devoted to satirizing the images of consumerism and corporate media. His targets: alcohol, fashion, automobiles, and fast food, to name a few. His Buy Nothing Day advert even made it onto CNN.

Examples? How about a vodka bottle that

slouches to one side. Under it, the words: ABSOLUTE IMPOTENCE. Or take Joe Chemo the smoking camel, lying in his deathbed, staring forlornly down at his sunglasses. Lasn also has begun marketing alternatives, such as the "Unswoosher," a shoe manufactured by well-paid workers, manufactured from 100 percent organic hemp and recycled tires, with a hand-drawn logo on the side and "sweet spot" on the toe . . . built for giving "toxic megacorporations what they truly need the most: a swift kick in the brand."

Lasn is not just fun and games, though. He has a dead-serious message: our consumer culture is destroying our values, our bodies, and our world. Take a few minutes today and check out the *Adbusters* Web site (www.adbusters.org) for a fun and thought-provoking examination of what the TV has been teaching us all these years. Or check out his book: *Culture Jam: How to Reverse America's Suicidal Consumer Binge—And Why We Must.*

Wearing Fairness on Your Sleeve

Being lectured to about garment-industry sweatshops is about as necessary these days as arguing against apartheid was in 1990. Everybody with a pulse gets it. A 2006 Harris poll said as much: 75 percent of Americans want Congress to ban sweatshop-made imports.

Numbers like those have had an impact. During the 1990s, some prominent apparel corporations were publicly shamed for using sweatshops. Kathie Lee Gifford was reduced to tears when confronted by activists over her use of sweatshops for her clothing line. Bad PR leads to slumping sales, so some made an effort to clean up their act. It's been an important victory, but it's estimated that only 10 percent of corporate abusers have made even a little effort.

Time to up the pressure.

If you're a clothes hound, do a little sniffing around. There's no labeling program for clothes, as there is for coffee. But you might start by asking if your favorite clothing stores are members of the Fair Trade Federation or registered as a fair trade organization. You can also check out the online store of your favorite brand. If they aren't members of the Fair Trade Federation, ask them why they're not. Let them know that you love their brand, but you'd love it even more if their clothes were made by safe, healthy, unionized workers, paid a living wage.

Even easier is to search out fair trade companies. Many of these businesses actually sell organic cotton products and cooperative-made clothes. The variety of clothing is quite surprising. Two good sources are union-made No Sweat Apparel at www.nosweatapparel.com and trend-setting, sweatshop-free American Apparel at www.americanapparel.net.

Be a walking advertisement for fair trade, not sweatshops. Just Do It.

Forest Wipe Out

Many folks have inadvertently become domestic lumberjacks, and their kitchens clear-cutting operations. Paper towels to wipe the counter, paper towels for the microwave, paper towels under the dog bowl, paper towels as napkins . . . Timmmberrr!

You can save trees in the kitchen by replacing paper towels with cloth towels. You're probably thinking: "But then I have to worry about where the towels have been." Here's a solution. Buy three separately colored or patterned sets of kitchen towels. Use one for drying dishes and your clean hands, one for wiping up the counter and table surfaces, and one for floor spills. Or devise your own system (a different Japanese anime character for each chore?). Whatever works.

One thing is clear: your impact on the world's forests will be lightened significantly. Plus, you'll save rivers from the bleaching of wood pulp to make the paper towels white—and save a few bucks per month. And if you fall into the Paul Bunyan camp of paper-towel users, that's a giant improvement!

Gearhead Greening

It's no secret that our cars pollute. But our car *parts* can be just as bad. Ever seen (or smelled) a tire fire? How about the deadly mess leaking out of a discarded car battery? Or a black stream of petrol goo running into the storm drain?

When it comes to car parts, we should all be green grease monkeys. Take the extra steps to dispose of your car parts and fluids appropriately: here's how.

Most garages will take your old tires off your hands when you're ready for new ones (also see Keep on Truckin', p. 260, on retreading tires). Some garages even offer a discount on your replacements when you recycle.

Car–battery pollution is so onerous that most states have enacted laws requiring you to recycle them. The result: only a small percentage go unrecycled. All that lead, sulfuric acid, and plastic stays out of the landfill and gets reused. Yeah! Ask auto-parts stores and garages to recycle them for you. Or, if needed, contact your local waste management agency.

Finally, there's your car's lifeblood: oil. Since oil is changed often, it's good to have a storage method worked out if you choose to do it yourself. It's not difficult. Simply keep your used motor oil in a tightly sealed and labeled plastic container (milk containers work well). Keep it stored safely until you're ready to take it into any oil-changing place. They'll recycle it for you.

None of
the Above

IMAGINE A RESTAURANT with a smallish menu, but no matter what you order, you're forced to eat the one dish the majority of customers order, which almost always turns out to be either Spam or Twinkies. You'd better pick the least awful of the two choices and hope everyone else does too, right? Actually, you'd probably just walk out, and so would just about everyone else.

Only a prize moron would run a restaurant like that. And yet, that's exactly how the U.S. election system is run. No wonder we've suffered under so many politicians who are either yellow-bellied, soft-centered sponges or pork-barrel, overcooked hams. Show me the exit!

But hold on. In places like Australia and even our very own San Francisco, voters are given a more logical choice. They get Instant Runoff Voting (IRV)— a system in which voters rank the candidates in order of preference. If your first choice doesn't have the votes to win, your vote goes to your second pick, and so forth, until there's a winner. That way, a vote for vegan gumbo or smart-chops is never wasted. Plus, IRV cuts out the costs of runoff elections, which often cost millions of dollars. Other places, such as Spain and Nevada, have a space on the ballot for "None of the Above" (NOTA). If NOTA gets a majority of votes, a new election is called.

Petition your newspaper or local candidate, or write a blog to tell management you're sick of junk politics only.

EZ Theoretical Action

The collective "Doh!" continues to roll across Florida. Somewhere in the vicinity of five hundred lapsed voters missed their chance to change the world (in theory, at least). Sure, thousands were illegitimately blocked from voting through aggressive voter roll purging and racial profiling. But nearly 30 percent of Floridians didn't even try. Given all the environmental and social setbacks, not to mention a notable resource war in Iraq, that's gotta hurt.

It's a fact that you can't vote if you're not registered with your local Office of Elections. But registering takes only about five minutes of your time. That's small peanuts when you consider all the long nights murmuring, "shoulda, woulda, coulda."

Registering is even easier than ever. At www. eac.gov there is an easily downloadable registration application. Your local DMV can register you the next time you get your license renewed. Simply ask to register. Local, state, or city offices, libraries, schools, and post offices are packed with registration materials around election time. And by the way, if you're already registered but have moved, you'll need to reregister.

And often during election season, local organizations like the League of Women Voters will dispatch representatives to street corners and in front of retail outlets in the hopes of getting people to sacrifice five minutes to register. Hey, that's 50 percent of ten minutes!

So if you're over eighteen, a U.S. citizen, and have a valid ID, you can play a role in the next election.

(Again, this is all in theory.)

Fair-Weather Vegan

Most likely, you know what "vegan" means. But just in case you don't, a loose definition is: anything made without any animal products. Sure, some folks split hairs: like, does the yeast in your beer count as animals? But pretty much everyone agrees that milk, cheese, and eggs are all animal products.

Here's some important facts: a vegan diet can load you up with complete proteins, virtually eliminate LDL (bad) cholesterol, pack you full of calcium and iron, and *taste great*!

It can also save you loads of cash, make washing your dishes *way* easier, improve your BO, keep your innards, er . . . moving smooth, and bring you closer to Einstein (okay, maybe not that last one). Did we mention it *tastes great*?

Veganism can also cut down on greenhouse gases, make life a lot better for animals, feed starving kids, help family farms stay in business—*and taste GREAT*!

Notice a theme here?

Now how about what vegan food is *not*. Vegan food is not what lame hippies who live for a blander world eat. Good-tasting vegan food can be as greasy, sweet, chocolaty, spicy, or salty as you want. It's that simple.

Check out the gals at How It All Vegan at ww.govegan.net for delicious recipes and try it out for a day. Or more simply, have that all-American vegan dish for lunch: the PB and J sandwich.

Bottled Water Blues

A lot of people think it's a shame that tap water is so polluted, and they're often right. But bottled water *ain't* the way out.

Not that long ago, there was local, clean tap water to drink just about everywhere in the United States. But as time passed, mines, farms, factories, and so forth polluted local water sources. Next thing you know, the bright guys in marketing whipped up a survey that said lots of us were scared about our water. So the big boss went out and got the rights to water from way off yonder that used to be free to the people who lived there.

Ta-da! Bottled water to save the day! Now we can all make believe everything's okay, and we've solved a problem, right?

Past the hype, bottled water looks like this: tons of studies show that it usually tastes no better than tap water. It costs more than gasoline, and its transportation cost will just keep going up. A lot of the same junk you're scared of is in bottled water, and labeling requirements are minimal. Plus, those plastic bottles leach carcinogenic xenoestrogens into the water. And the bottles themselves are a source of *stupendous* volumes of waste and pollution.

The real water choice is either paying corporate hacks to abscond with someone's *possibly* clean water or taking responsibility and dealing with the pollution of our local water.

In the meantime, you can use a good, cheap water filter for your home.

Dust in the Wind

A less-than-mediocre, geographically named 1970s faux-progressive-rock outfit popularized the idea that all we are is "Dust in the Wind."

Unfortunately, we *will* be dust if we don't do something to halt global warming ASAP. If you're reading this book, you're probably already aware of the dangers of CO_2 emissions and greenhouse gases. But to truly keep us from becoming said windblown dust, we must focus on dust.

Yes, dust. As in feather-duster dust.

See, keeping your bulbs dust-free will help you realize that that 60-watt bulb is much too bright. A dusty one won't beam as brightly as it is meant to.

Once you get in the habit of dusting your light sources, you'll be able to cut back on bulb wattage, power, and energy: all leading to less CO_2 emitted from your electric power company.

Essentially, you will be helping to prevent the greenhouse effect *and* any potential for incessant, mass radio play of the aforementioned ditty when the apocalypse does indeed become imminent.

While you're dusting off your prospects for survival, it's also wise to keep your heating vents well dusted. It's all in the name of energy efficiency and better listening pleasure!

Low-Impact Gardening

EUROPEAN PLANTS SUCK. Suck water, that is. Across North America, popular European grasses, flowers, and bushes use more water than the local environment can supply. It has been estimated that Americans use 34 percent more water than is replaced by rainfall and runoff. The result is declining watersheds, saltwater intrusion, and sinking cities that jeopardize the health of our communities.

In response, water-saving gardening techniques have been developed to create landscapes in cities and around homes that work with local conditions. These strategies can be applied not just by lawn lovers in Las Vegas, but also by people from muggy Mississippi to lake-blessed Minnesota.

The following water-saving tips can be applied to any garden.

1. Consider your water-saving options. How big should your lawn be? What species are best?
2. Learn about your local soil conditions. Does it need help holding water?

3. Look into the native species of your area (or similar geographic areas).
4. Design your irrigation to be efficient—no sprinklers watering the sidewalk!
5. Use mulch to reduce soil temperature and evaporation.

Remember, being a water-conscious gardener does not mean tearing out your lawn in favor of rocks and cactus. Sunny California, for example, has kindred climates in Australia, South Africa, Chile, and Italy, each with wonderful species that can be found at your local nursery. The point is: you can still have the green without all the wet. More information can be found at www.xeriscape.org.

Rock Your Town

In the fall of 1988, a little-known band from LA rocked a small armpit club in Las Vegas packed full of unsuspecting teenagers. The act was the unknown, soon-to-be sensational Janes Addiction. Needless to say, the show was worth the three bucks.

It's not always a Las Vegas punk show jackpot, but supporting local music—from community orchestras to your local hip-hop crew—is one of the best ways to have fun and be an integral part of your community. Local musicians usually don't get rich. They do it for the love. And that love requires a partner: you.

Community orchestras are generally regular folks who take the time to practice after work or school so they can play for people in the community. Just as important is the local rock or hip-hop scene, where kids do a lot of growing up and adults try to stay young. Often local bands go on tour. That five-buck door cover can help the musicians get to the next town. And going over to their table to purchase their CD can help pay the rent. You might even see the next Green Day or Elvis in the coziness of your neighborhood bar.

Oh, and if you choose to stay home, please don't call the cops the next time the neighbor kids sponsor a band in their backyard. Give 'em a break. Go see a movie, or even better, go next door and rock out with them.

Puppeteering Change

The tired, traditional toolbox of political action seems so twentieth century. Handing out flyers, making countless phone calls, going door-to-door, all of these are simply drowned in the information tide of our digital age. Petitioning might have won American independence, but today, canvassing the old-fashioned way is more likely to generate sleep than salvation.

So how to generate awareness? And how to do it on the cheap?

There's a tool available to the public for free that facilitates sharing ideas, rallying your allies, and disseminating information that can help bring about local, national, or global change. It's called e-mail.

Okay, you're probably asking yourself: "How much political spam did I just flush down my computer's toilet?"

But the truth is, e-mail is still the most efficient way to reach people. You just have to be creative. E-mail revolutionaries requiring inspiration need look no further than giant puppets. That's right, puppets—big silly ones. Check out any major urban protest. You'll see a thousand signs lost in the crowd, but then here come the giant puppets of well-loathed, tarred-and-feathered political figures. Hey, you can't miss that!

There's no formula to making "giant puppets" of your e-mail. You can just add color to your text, change the fonts here and there, add photos, or, for the truly daring, learn some HTML or Flash to liven up your message. However you do it, the next shot heard round the world must be heard, so let it out with a *bang*!

Whistle-blowing While You Work

It just got harder to be the Good Samaritan. In a five-to-four decision in *Garcetti v. Ceballos*, the U.S. Supreme Court held that government whistle-blowers are not protected from employer retribution when an employee alerts the public to government wrongdoing. That's good news for government fraudsters and pork barrel politicos, and bad news for everyone else. But don't count on this stopping future whistle-blowing.

People just love turning in the boss. In fact, whistle-blowers often become the stuff of legends. Some have their lives turned into Oscar-nominated movies like *The Insider, North Country* and *Silkwood.* Some become historical icons like FBI whistleblower W. Mark Felt, aka Deep Throat. Some become local folk heroes like Police Officer Frank Serpico, who exposed corruption in the NYPD. Whistle-blowers have done everything from exposing lying politicians to alerting the public to dangerous polluters and identifying sexual harassment at work.

The bad news is that many whistle-blowers get hurt. The good news is the world is made better by whistle-blowers' actions. If you notice wrongdoing at work and are compelled to take a stand, there are a few organizations that can help you. The National Whistleblower Center at www.whistleblowers.org is a good resource for learning the law about whistle-blowing. Whistle-blower extraordinaire Daniel Ellsberg has also put together the Truth-Telling Project with the ACLU to help government workers. And some institutions honor whistle-blowers—including The Nation Institute's Ron Riddenhour Awards (www.ridenhour.org).

Be the Farmer

If you ever wanted to own a farm but hated the thought of getting up before dawn every day, there's a modern alternative that won't disturb your beauty sleep. With the system known as community supported agriculture (CSA), members of a community partner with a local farm and reap the bounty. That means fresh, often organic produce, grown in season and delivered to your house every week. Just like a real farmer enjoys!

CSAs began in the 1960s in Japan, when outraged mothers responded to the arsenic poisoning of twelve thousand infants by powdered milk, six hundred of whom died. The mothers organized and formed *teikei*, or alliances, with area farmers to provide fresh milk for their families. Simultaneously, Europeans began forming CSAs, which eventually found purchase in the United States in 1986.

Today, American CSAs have spread to over 1,000 farms. There are two kinds of CSAs. One variety offers consumers an agreed-upon price for the whole season, sharing both the farm's produce and the risks and rewards with the farmer. The other variation offers consumers weekly subscriptions with prices set by the farmer, who solely takes on the risks and rewards. Some CSAs even operate as corporations, where consumers own shares and maintain the farm through hired farmers.

However you do it, CSAs benefit both the consumer and the farmer. Many offer organic produce, meat, dairy products, and even flowers. And since the middlemen are cut out, CSAs can be a cheaper way to get organic fruits and vegetables.

Check out www.localharvest.org for a complete list of CSAs in your area.

Keep on Truckin'

Truckers are experts in a lot of things besides where to get the best chili on Route 66. The next time you sally up to the diner counter after a long drive, pick the brain of the trucker next to you. You'll probably learn a thing or two: like how many lives a tire has.

It takes around eight gallons of oil to produce one passenger vehicle tire. A retreaded tire of the same size will take two to three gallons. According to the Tire Retread Information Bureau, North Americans currently save four hundred million barrels of oil a year by retreading their tires.

Currently, truck and other commercial vehicle tires represent two thirds of the tires retreaded, because most truckers will try every which way but loose when it comes to their costs. They'll tell you how they save up to 50 percent of what a new tire would cost. And retreads perform just as well as new, and they're just as safe, too.

But here's the catch: only 15 percent of tires are accepted for retreading. You see, a tire's casing is a complex tube that must be cared for. Most people don't treat their tires well enough to get them retreaded. But if you keep your tires properly inflated and maintained retreading is possible.

Check out www.retread.org for more info on proper tire care.

So how many lives *does* a tire have? Five, if you do them right. That's a big 10-4, good buddy.

Rag Time

IF YOU THINK your period is a pain for you, you should see what it's doing to the planet. The greatest myth about tampon applicators is the term "flushable" or "biodegradable" found on the label of the box. In actuality, tampons end up in our landfills and sewage systems and ultimately in the ocean. During

1998 and 1999, over 170,000 tampon applicators were collected along U.S. coastal areas. Some were even found in the stomachs of sea birds.

Also, the synthetic fibers and chemicals used to produce the cotton in feminine products are both harmful to our environment and to the health of women who use these products. The cotton used to make tampons and pads is treated with pesticides, fertilizers, defoliants, and herbicides including cyanide, dicofol, naled, propargite, and trifluralin.

Here are some tips to protect yourself and your environment: don't flush tampons or applicators. Avoid lubricated and fragranced products or products with plastic applicators and plastic liners. Instead, try organic, biodegradable pads and tampons, grown naturally, without harmful chemicals.

Alternatively, you could try washable pads. And then there are menstrual cups made of silicone or rubber, which can last up to ten years, making them the most eco-friendly of all the products (they are not recommended for virgins).

While your period will still be a monthly downer, at least the world's water systems and marine creatures won't go down the drain, too.

Green Slaughter

"Don't drink and slime." Despite the warning, millions of snails and slugs are killed every year doing just that. The dirty business starts, well, in the dirt; around sunken milk cartons, cut in half and filled with a little beer. Those party-loving mollusks can't resist the lure of all that yummy microbrew and just fall right in.

It's bloody business, but even the most passive of us must wage war in our own gardens. But why kill all the friendlies in the process? Smart green gardeners don't have to resort to weapons of mass destruction. There are more diplomatic alternatives available.

Green pest control can be as simple as planting strong-smelling herbs such as basil and parsley next to your vegetables. Bugs can't stand the stuff. And if retrieving the spent shells of beer-drowned snails isn't to your liking, you can sprinkle irritating sawdust around your plants to protect them. Keeping a pet duck around to do the evil deed is another alternative.

Here are some more green recipes for pest-disaster:

- Weed spray: make a spray of neem (a tree root) or pyrethrum (a flower) to use on marauding weeds. Careful you don't spray the good guys, though.
- Aphids: soak six garlic cloves in two pints of water for a few days and filter. Use it directly on aphid colonies. Alternatively, mix one part espresso with ten parts water.
- Personal insect repellent: use citronella or lavender oil. Alternatives include lemongrass or lemon thyme; take your pick.

Boy Buys Hammer, Saves Town

The cashier is determined to give you customer satisfaction, right after she finishes reciting all the scripted questions from corporate. When that's done, she'll take your money and send it out of your community to a boardroom far, far away. Thank you for shopping at Sprawl-Mart.

Nostalgic for the days when downtown was vibrant and slow talk over the register was done on a first-name basis? Back when money changed hands and stayed right there in your community? Sadly, many communities have lost that kind of commerce. Big chains have been beating local commercial centers to death for decades. The statistics aren't pretty. The death toll in the United States in the 1990s alone was: five thousand local hardware stores, ten thousand local pharmacies, and two thousand local bookstores. This has been bad news not only for cordial shopping, but also for the livelihood of our cities and towns.

In a classic examination of local economics known as the Andersonville Study, researchers discovered that local businesses recirculate nearly $7 out of $10 back into the local economy. Only $4.30 stayed locally when it was spent at a chain store.

So is there anything a concerned shopper can do? Yes. Shop local and buy directly. Local businesses are still around and often outdo their big box competitors. And you probably won't stump the sales clerk with technical questions. You can shop at local flea markets, farmers' markets, and garage sales, too.

Do your town right today and swagger over to your local store for a fair exchange.

Guessing Game

The day before we invented the wheel, a spiritual insight was hatched. Ever since, all the great teachers have understood that humans consist of four parts: heart, mind, body, and spirit. Your heart feels, your mind thinks, and your body moves. Your spirit is how you interact with everything in the universe that you can't know with your five senses or prove with your mind.

The day *after* the wheel was invented, someone wheeling by announced the next revelation: the great

teachers don't know everything. While enlighten-
ment doesn't come on the fly, you do have the power
to guess. What and how *you* guess is just as good
(and as right) as any guess by a teacher, your mom,
or even (gulp!) the pope.

Consequently, spirituality is not going to church,
converting your friends, feeling guilty, thinking about
God, reading a "holy" book, or abstaining from good
sex. It's more about finding the sacred in what you do.
If supporting small farms, feeding your children safe
food, and not buying junk brings you joy, then do
those things! And while you find joy, ask questions
like: "What's bigger: all I can see, or all I can't see?"
or, "What's sacred to me?" or, "What does 'spiritual'
mean?" Keep asking. Eventually, the answers will
start adding up.

Some find the sacred in family, others in friends, and
some in Elvis. Yes, Elvis! As in Elvis Uunderground:
The Church! (www.elvisunderground.org). But it's just
one guess among many.

And remember, Elvis loves you!

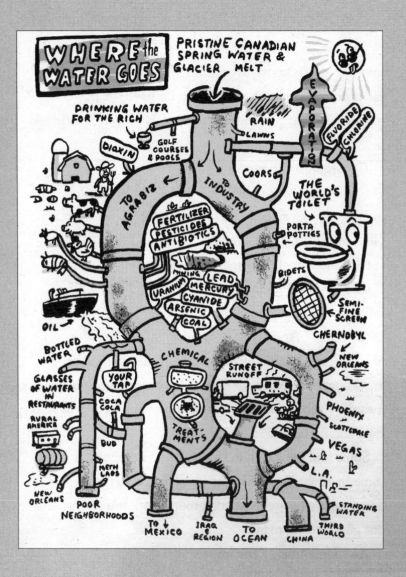

One Big, Wet Journey

Most of us are clear on water: it comes through our faucet and goes down the drain. But as Peggy Lee once asked: is that all there is? Not so long ago, every kid could answer that question, because they were the ones who hauled the water home. And they knew a lot more about where it went, because they hauled that, too.

When we know more about our water's journey, we can be better judges about how we use it and what we dump in it. Here's a rundown to get you started.

Water often comes to us from a reservoir. Other times, people dig wells to underground springs and then pump the water into a holding tank or right into a pipe network.

Once used, water goes down the drain into a wastewater system. If you have a septic tank, the waste sits there while the solids settle out, and then the liquids slowly seep out over a chunk of land called a leech field, where microbes make it safe. If you use a public sewer, the waste gets emptied somewhere (hopefully not your local river or ocean). It's supposed to be cleaned before they let it go.

You can often tour your local waterworks and wastewater plants. If you ask a few questions, like whether it comes from a reservoir or a well, and how the drinking water and wastewater are sanitized, you'll be your neighborhood expert and a good judge of how to use your water.

Paradigm Shift, Revisited

In the 1992 U.S. presidential election, Bill Clinton thrashed his opponent, George H. W. Bush, with the mantra, "It's the *economy*, stupid." Today, with global warming either poorly addressed or totally ignored, freshwater supplies getting scarcer, energy costs skyrocketing, and corporate graft and power rising, a new mantra is in order. We posit the following: "It's the *paradigm*, stupid."

The paradigm suggested by *The Ten Minute Activist* is not a new one, but it still rings true: small, individual contributions add up. If we choose to, we can live as titans of principle, living lightly and happily, but moving the world nonetheless. Such is the sentiment of our final suggested action: to learn how beautiful, and powerful, *small* can be.

In 1973, E. F. Schumacher, a British economist, wrote his seminal work, *Small Is Beautiful.* Considered one of the most influential authors of the twentieth century, Schumacher outlined his vision of human-scaled economics and appropriate technologies. He devised a means to tame corporations and transform them into vehicles of both profit and social progress. And he developed ways to respond to poverty and modern alienation. Many of his ideas were adopted into real-world solutions from India to Great Britain, and from Chile to California.

Small Is Beautiful may be the next book you read,

or may be your favorite new slogan. Either way, Schumacher's paradigm is still timely and can still inspire.

Live small and prosper.

The Mission Collective

ONDINE BLACK is a literary agent, poet, and amateur astrologer who worked on this book because she wanted to read it.

M RYAN HESS spends his time plunging his fingers in as many pies as possible. From blogging to film-making to writing, he has lived and traveled in over thirty countries, generating three documentary films and a series of articles.

IAN KNOX is a musician, filmmaker, and freelance writer. He was recently voted MVP of San Francisco's Mission Baseball League.

JAY KULLMAN is a photographer, a New Orleans native, a political junkie, avid naturalist, and music addict.

DEACON RIVERS is a leading Zen commando and scholar of punk spirituality and pirate religion. With vast wealth of knowledge in information science, communications, mass media, entheogenics, remergent technologies, global trade, and resource accounting. Deacon Rivers is both very successful and popular, counting friends, colleagues, and students by thousands, and is a founding member of Elvis underground: The Church!

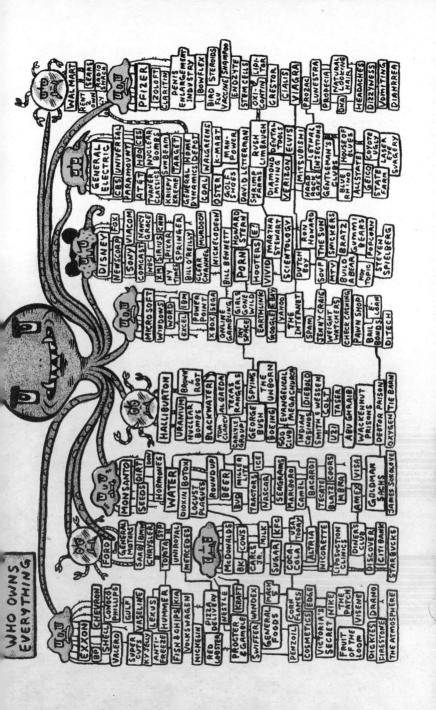

The Illustrator

LLOYD DANGLE is a writer, designer, and artist whose work has appeared in over 100 magazines and newspapers. His comic strip, *Troubletown,* is a widely-syndicated cartoon feature in alternative newsweeklies, and he is universally recognized for drawing the cartoons on packages of Airborne, the world's number-one cold remedy.

www.tenminuteactivist.com

www.lloyddangle.com

www.troubletown.com